It's Just Your Imagination
Growing Up with a Narcissistic Mother – Insights of a Personal Journey

Revital Shiri-Horowitz

Copyright © 2017 Revital Shiri-Horowitz

All rights reserved, including the right to reproduce this book or portions there of in any form whatsoever. For information please contact the author directly.

Editor: Shlomit Lica
Publisher: Horowitz Publishing

ISBN-13:
978-1-64204-729-5

TABLE OF CONTENTS

ACKNOWLEDGMENTS	vi
INTRODUCTION	1
PART ONE	3
ON SHAME AND IMAGINATION - GROWING UP AS THE DAUGHTER OF A NARCISSISTIC MOTHER	
CHAPTER ONE	4
CHAPTER TWO	17
CHAPTER THREE	21
CHAPTER FOUR	28
CHAPTER FIVE	33
CHAPTER SIX	37
CHAPTER SEVEN	43
PART TWO	44
HOW DID I AVOID TURNING INTO MY MOTHER?	
CHAPTER EIGHT	45
CHAPTER NINE	50
CHAPTER TEN	54
CHAPTER ELEVEN	58
CHAPTER TWELVE	61
PART THREE	69
AWARENESS, GROWTH, AND COPING MECHANISMS	
CHAPTER THIRTEEN	70
CHAPTER FOURTEEN	73
CHAPTER FIFTEEN	76
CHAPTER SIXTEEN	79
PART FOUR	82
THE ROAD TO RECOVERY – UNDERSTANDING, ACCEPTANCE, AND RECONCILIATION	
CHAPTER SEVENTEEN	83
CHAPTER EIGHTEEN	84
CHAPTER NINETEEN	91
CHAPTER TWENTY	95
CHAPTER TWENTY-ONE	98
ABOUT THE AUTHOR	137

ACKNOWLEDGMENTS

I would like to thank Dr. Karyl McBride, therapist and couples and family counselor, who has been working for more than thirty years in her clinic for trauma victims, and whose primary field of research is narcissism. Her first book, "Will I Ever be Good Enough? Healing the Daughters of Narcissistic Mothers," is dedicated to daughters of narcissistic mothers.

With the help of her book, McBride opened my eyes and accompanied me along my path. I could not have gone through this process without it. McBride gave me permission to quote from it throughout my book.

A special thank you to the man who is by my side through good and bad, joy and sorrow, wealth and poverty. I was blessed with a life-long friend.

Thank you to my cousins Michal Yekutiely and Ofra Sofri, friends through both childhood and adulthood, for their support and unconditional love. Thanks to my wonderful friends who supported me, lovingly pushed me, affirmed me, and helped me believe in myself: Michal Lapid, Galit Arad-Trutner, Yafit Haba, Hagit Kfir, and Michal Khen of blessed memory.

INTRODUCTION
The Mother in your Head and the Mother in your Heart

When you hear the word "Mother," what thoughts come to mind? For me, *mother* is a complicated word. A mother is supposed to be warm and protective, always thinking about the wellbeing of her children, her chicks; they are always foremost in her mind. So, what was it like to grow up with a different kind of mother, a mother who puts herself before her children?

Today, I can understand her behavior from a rational perspective, but my feelings towards her continue to be very complex. There is the mother in my head and the mother in my heart, and between the two there are countless feelings of guilt. What I mean by "the mother in the head and the mother in the heart" is the realization that something isn't right. We – the daughters – are getting mixed messages from the "mother in the head," whereas we feel only love towards "the mother in the heart," even as we sense that something is "off" in her love for us. But I'm getting ahead of myself. Let's take it slowly.

There are many phrases that express the importance of the mother in our culture: "we only have one mother," "there's nothing like a mom's love," etc. The subject of mothers is still taboo in our culture, and if a daughter says something that is perceived as defiant towards her mother, the reaction she gets is something along the lines of "You must be misunderstanding your mother" or "That's impossible, a mother always loves her children." Some of the responses may even be excruciatingly sharp:

"Your mother did everything for you, how dare you talk about her that way?" These kinds of reactions cause these daughters – who aren't self-confident to begin with and whose grasp of the world feels shaky – to believe that there's something wrong with them.

This book was written with the blood of my heart, amidst an internal war against feelings of guilt, a fear of hurting her, and the knowledge that I would be placing myself on the front lines. I have no doubt that this book shatters the myth of motherhood, and at the same time, as a writer, I want to approach these girls and unambiguously tell them, "It's not you, it's your mothers."

There are unemphatic mothers (this is a type of borderline disability disorder), and there are mothers who compete with, or envy, their daughters. And no, it is not the mothers' fault, because chances are they themselves grew up with these kinds of mothers and didn't receive the love they needed. As a result, they only have a vague grasp of what love really is, and are limited in how much love they can give and receive. It is important to say these things outright, and not to sweep them under the rug.

I wrote this book to address the issue of narcissistic mothers and their daughters. It strives to help these daughters understand that they are adequate, that what they have been feeling and experiencing for so many years is real, and that there are other women who share their emotions. They are not aberrant, and they are not alone.

The goal of this book is to share my experience, along with the insights I've amassed over the years, both from articles I've read and from my own therapy. I don't presume to label this a psychology textbook; I have no training in that field. I just want to tell my own story, in the hope that it will help other women like me.

PART ONE
ON SHAME AND IMAGINATION - GROWING UP AS THE DAUGHTER OF A NARCISSISTIC MOTHER

CHAPTER ONE
What is Narcissism?

The word "narcissism" comes from the story of Narcissus, a handsome Greek demigod who was beloved by men and women alike, but didn't love anyone else in return. Ultimately, he fell in love with his own reflection. People with a narcissistic disorder are unable to see other people, much less to show them empathy. From their perspective, the world is there to serve their needs. They are unable to understand other people's pain, and they put themselves at the center regardless of the cost. In my case, this meant that if something happened in my life, it didn't matter unless it was in my mother's best interests.

What is a narcissistic mother?

Most narcissistic mothers were raised by narcissistic mothers. Their condition doesn't emanate from any one source; it is something that developed over many years. These mothers never learned another way of relating to their children, and they didn't have the skills or knowledge to raise their children differently. Narcissism, which is considered a borderline mental disorder rather than a mental illness, is characterized by a person's belief that the world is part of that person, and its entire purpose is to serve him or her. The children of narcissistic women do not exist as separate entities; they are part of their mothers, and so the mothers have the absolute right to manipulate them so that they meet her needs. Without her, they don't exist.

In one of my more difficult conversations with my mother, she shouted at me, "But you're mine!" I was already in my fifties at the time, a grown woman, and I understood that I was a separate and independent entity. I paused for a moment, and, not wanting to offend her, said, "I don't belong to you or to anyone else. I belong to myself." Perhaps this sounds childish, but in this conversation, as in so many others, I made a point of drawing a dividing line between us. She has said it many times since then, whenever she feels that I don't understand that my role is to be with her, do something for her, or be the same person as her. The feeling I get when she says those kinds of things is hard to put into words.

I am not anyone else's property. I don't belong to her. I'm a person with feelings, desires, and dreams that have absolutely nothing to do with my mother. So how can I "be hers?"

My mother never drew a line between us, unless she was hurting or insulting me. At those times, she would separate herself from me. Most of the time, though, she had no problem searching through my bedroom closets and taking any clothes that struck her fancy. If I'm hers, everything I own is hers, too. I am her, she is me, and what belongs to me belongs to her. A lack of boundaries is one of the more difficult problems facing the daughters of narcissistic mothers.

Fundamental memories

Memories are a delicate weave of the many moments that made us who we are. Fundamental memories are the memories that instill within us something that we carry throughout our lives. Every person grows up in a unique family, in a unique atmosphere, and our experiences over the course of our lives help shape who we are today. I grew up as my parents' oldest child; a son and another daughter were born after me. I remember an unpredictable childhood with an unpredictable mother and a father who was absent even when he was there.

One of my fundamental memories is of Yom Kippur in my

grandparents' house in Lod, outside Tel Aviv. I am six or seven years old. My mother decides that I must fast until morning because I'm already a big girl. It doesn't take long for me to become hungry and thirsty; I want to break my fast, but my mother gets angry, so angry. Her words are hurtful and humiliating: "You can't restrain yourself! You just ate, now shut your mouth and go to sleep." Feeling mortified, I try to still my hunger pangs. My grandmother sees this, quietly takes me into her bedroom, and gives me a vegetable pastry. It quiets my stomach, and I can fall asleep.

My mother was a master of enchantment. She could "magically" ensure that when we returned home from Shabbat at our grandparents' house, our beds were already made. She was dynamic and full of energy, and we were lucky enough to have all kinds of unusual experiences. We would wake up in the morning and take the train to Netanya, for no reason; we would picnic under the eucalyptus trees before heading home. She was a person who delighted in unexpected experiences, always unexpected, for better or for worse. My mother was our queen. She knew everything, and she knew it best.

I'm sure I didn't say the right thing at the right time. Her usual response was to grab my hands, pick me up, and throw me on the cold floor. "I'm not your mother, and I don't want to see your face," she would say. "Get out of here." This wasn't a one-time event; it happened repeatedly, not just towards me but towards my siblings as well. To this day, this gesture and the words that went with it cause me pain, as if they have pierced my heart with a knife. Now that I am a mother myself, I can never understand this behavior, this rejection. A child is not an object; you don't throw it on the floor, not physically and not emotionally.

For many years, I had terrible rages. I always felt that my mother wanted to control me and everything that was mine. She considered this manipulation a manifestation of maternal love. I told myself that her controlling nature was proof of her love, of her concern. I was unable to look at the situation with cool objectivity and see the painful truth: my mother claimed me for herself when it suited her, and kicked me out into the world when

I didn't meet her expectations.

Mixed messages

Intuitively, I understood that something was not right, but I couldn't put my finger on what that something was. On the one hand, I was getting the message that I was undeserving of love, and on the other hand, I was hearing things that sounded a little like love. As a girl, I found this terribly confusing. Daughters of narcissistic mothers have experiences that other daughters can't understand. After all, don't all mothers love their children unconditionally? Aren't they all protective and even-tempered, supportive and helpful? A mother is not supposed to be manipulative and hurtful. She's supposed to be a stabilizing force, not a disorienting one, someone who makes her children stronger, not weaker. She's not supposed to leave her children emotionally stranded. Daughters of narcissistic mothers grow up on shaky ground – they never know if the things that are said to them are true, or if they're just being manipulated yet again. What is true and what isn't? And what will set their mother off again? These daughters are growing up with a profound sense of instability.

I have no doubt that even narcissistic mothers – our mothers – are trying their best, but their best is limited, and the results are painful. What is even harder is what happens when we become mothers ourselves.

What is love?

How do we bestow love? How do we learn to be attuned to our children when our own mothers weren't attuned to us? What is maternal love? And what is marital love? How do we know when we love someone? How do we know when someone loves us back, unconditionally, simply for being who we are? These are some of the questions that this book will address, questions I continue to struggle with to this day.

I am already past fifty, and it is still hard for me to believe that someone loves me simply because I am me. I define love as a given, as the desire to make another person happy without expecting anything in return. This is what I call "groundless love" – such simple words, yet they comprise the entire world.

Daughters of narcissistic mothers don't think they deserve love, and they do not fully believe that their partners, or even their children, love them unconditionally.

This, I believe, is the primary struggle for these daughters. What is love, really? Are we truly deserving of love? And how do we love those who are close to us?

As a young mother, I felt a tremendous amount of love towards my children, which manifested itself in my desire to protect them and to always be a few steps ahead of them so I could anticipate their needs. Moreover, I had an inexplicable fear that I wouldn't recognize the signs of a physical or emotional problem. That I wouldn't pay attention, *really* pay attention, to their emotional and physical needs. This fear has been a constant motif in the raising and education of my four sons.

This fear – of overlooking an emotional or physical problem, of unintentionally ignoring something, of lacking empathy, of not being there when they needed me – haunts me every day. I am constantly "taking inventory" to make sure that everything is all right. Even with my children who are out of the house and no longer need my help on a daily basis, I continue to be on the lookout for anything I might have missed. I always thought this trait was common to all mothers, but now I realize that this is not the case. It seems I am the exception.

Anyone who hasn't suffered from emotional neglect will struggle to understand my behavior. Now that I've read the articles, taken myself in hand, and gone through the process of grief, acknowledgement and acceptance, I can tell you that the need to protect, to nurture, to be attuned to the needs of others, continues to besiege me. I live with the fear that narcissism will somehow attach itself to me. Its rudiments exist inside me, and if I am not strong enough to break the chain, I will pass it down to my children, just as I received it from my mother, who received it from hers.

A dynasty of narcissistic mothers

My grandmother didn't know how to love, nor did my mother. My grandmother was a smart woman who knew how to use people to her advantage. She was born in Iraq, the first daughter to survive after the loss of several infants. She was the apple of her father's eye; as far as he was concerned, she was second only to God. To him, she was a queen, a celestial being. He worshiped her, and would do anything she wished. She was one of the few Iraqi girls who learned to read and write in the beginning of the twentieth century.

My grandmother liked to tell me about her father. In contrast, she revealed very little about her relationship with her mother. She told me more than once that her mother was a fool, and didn't interest her at all. Essentially, my grandmother served as a surrogate for her own mother, becoming her father's platonic wife: she was his daughter, his wife, and his confidante. He consulted with her and gave her whatever he could. I am sure he never imagined that he was raising a little monster who thought that she deserved everything and the whole world revolved around her.

My grandfather had grown up fatherless. His father had gone to fight in the First World War and returned many years later, a broken vessel. During the war, and the years that followed, his mother supported her small family, with my grandfather – her eldest son – at her side (I wrote about these years in my book "Daughter of Iraq" [1]) When the time came for her to choose a husband, she married my grandfather, who knew enough to give her whatever her heart desired. My grandfather treated my grandfather like a queen, and took upon himself certain tasks that most of the men of his time would have shunned; he was the one, for example, who bathed the children. Everything was fine while they lived in Iraq, but when they came to Israel and my grandfather couldn't meet all the needs of his queen, my grandmother turned

---

[1] Daughter of Iraq, Revital Shiri Horowitz, Gevanim, Israel 2007

her back on him and turned her children against him.

She decided that now it was her oldest son's role to meet all her needs, even though he was already in charge of all his younger siblings. She sat at home while they worked, cleaned, did the laundry – anything to appease their queen. Meanwhile, my grandmother used her free time to decorate her palace (first a tent in the desert, then a tiny house), to take indulgent vacations, and to go to the beauty salon. It never occurred to her children that they were doing anything out of the ordinary. After all, they were "trained" to obey their mother. They would continue to worship her for many years, until the death of my grandfather. Only then did the children understand what was really going on. This understanding, however, came too late. My grandfather never had a chance to receive his children's love. He did get a measure of love from his grandchildren, myself among them. I listened to him, and I was proud of my smart and kind grandfather. He influenced me deeply, even though he was not an ongoing presence in my life.

It was from him that I inherited my love for religion, for prayers and sacred texts. I'm a non-observant Jew, and I don't go to synagogue as faithfully as he did, but thanks to him, my roots are deep and strong.

Even without making his voice heard, my grandfather influenced me. I remember his tremendous *joie de vivre*, and his praise for God despite his difficult life. My grandfather was a man of work and of Torah. He worked in Tel Aviv until the last year of his life, when he got sick at the age of seventy-five. He and my grandmother lived just outside of Tel Aviv, in the city of Lod. He would get up early every day to pray, then take two buses to his job in Tel Aviv. He observed the Sabbath, as well as all the holidays, whether or not his family joined him. He was the reason I went to synagogue, as father was an atheist. My father honored my grandfather by occasionally accompanying him to synagogue, but even when he didn't go, I would sometimes attend. I remember a conversation I had with my grandfather soon before he died, in which he explained a biblical verse. "A wind can break rocks," he quoted. "Do you know what this verse means?" Of course I didn't. He explained to me that *Sla'eem,* the Hebrew word for rocks, is an acronym for the coalition of our five Arab adversaries: Syria, Lebanon, Iraq, Jordan and Egypt. "Wind," he said, "is the spirit of God, and it is strong enough to break SLA'EEM (סלעים) – the Hebrew word for "rocks." This was right after the Yom Kippur War. This is what my beloved grandfather said, and to this day, I remember how we used to sit next to each other and talk, and how impressed I was by his wisdom and knowledge. I must have been only about nine years old at the time, but there are some things you never forget, things you carry with you forever.

My mother grew up with a narcissistic mother; she didn't go through a process of blossoming, but remained hurt, and hurtful. She copied her mother's maternal paradigm, and, to my regret, her marital paradigm, too. She didn't know how to build a respectful, loving partnership. To her credit, it must be said that she didn't try to turn us against our father; that being said, she didn't teach us to love and respect him, either. Nonetheless, my siblings and I all had a loving relationship with him.

In my case, this love was fused with compassion and pity, for his weakness and his helplessness; I can't speak for my siblings. It's worth noting that none of us harbors any residual hate towards him. Apparently, we all forgave him for not fulfilling his role as a father. The truth is, we had very few expectations of him, because that's what our mother had taught us. She was the head, and he wasn't even the neck.

In the end, after years of exploring the concept of the dynasty of narcissistic mothers, my greatest fear was that I would continue the cycle. I am very aware of this, and I imagine that other daughters of narcissistic mothers feel the same way.

The relationship between, and characteristics of, narcissistic mothers and their daughters

In her book "Will I Ever be Good Enough?,"[2] author Karyl

---

[2] Dr. Karyl McBride is a therapist and a marriage and family counselor. For more than thirty years, she has been counseling trauma victims in her clinic. Her primary field of research is narcissism. Her first book, "Will I Ever be Good Enough:

McBride presents different archetypes of narcissistic mothers. According to McBride, these are the distinguishing characteristics of their daughters:

1) **You consistently try to earn your mother's love, attention, and affirmation, but you never succeed.** Narcissistic mothers have trouble accepting their daughters as they are, and are therefore constantly criticizing them. My mother told me dozens of times that I was fat. When we went shopping and I tried on an outfit, she looked at me with disgust and said, "Your body is unacceptable. You've got to do something about it."
Any time there was an opportunity for her to praise me, she would criticize me instead. If my success wasn't her success, it was irrelevant, insignificant to the point of non-existence. There were many times my successes weren't deemed worthy of acknowledgement: parties that never happened (or if they did happen, became hers), achievements that went unnoticed, and so on.

2) **Your mother is more concerned with how things look than with how they make you feel.** It was always very important to my mother to look wonderful to the outside world. It didn't matter how she felt, as long as she looked amazing. Because of my awkwardness (was I really awkward?), I struck my mother as a foreign species. Consequently, she often commented that I looked like my father's family. She told me that other people didn't have to know how I was really feeling; to the outside world, everything should always seem positive. "Not everyone has to know when you don't want to go somewhere, or when you're in a bad mood." Life was one

---

Healing the Daughters of Narcissistic Mothers", is dedicated to the daughters of narcissistic mothers.

big performance, and I was the supporting actor for the star – my mother.

3) **Your mother is jealous of you.** Most mothers want to be proud of their daughters, but narcissistic mothers see their daughters as competition. Every time you get attention, you're rewarded with your mother's anger or punishment or attempt to draw the attention over to herself. When I turned twelve, my mother organized a party "for me." The music wasn't to my taste, and while my mother danced in the center of the room, I was playing with my cousins in a different room. There was nothing about the party that was mine other than the fact that it was in my name. At my fourth son's Bar Mitzvah, my mother couldn't be there. I wasn't all that sad, because I knew that if she'd been there, all the attention would have been deflected from my son, his siblings, and his parents and onto her.

4) **Your mother doesn't respect your individuality or your independence, especially if it is in opposition to her wishes or threatens her in any way.** When I left home and moved in with my partner, my mother was furious. My boyfriend was going to throw me out, she yelled, and after that nobody would give me a second look. She also made a point of saying, "How can my daughter go live with her boyfriend after I told my sister that her son's girlfriend was promiscuous because she lives with him?" When I was drafted, I joined Nachal, a program that combines military service with agricultural work. For the first few months, my mother "excommunicated" me, and tried to divert me from my plan and force me to return home. For two entire years, every time we spoke on the telephone, my mother begged me to come home.

5) **Everything in your family is connected to your mother.** When I call my mother and ask her what's new, she tells me – in detail – about her day, her life, her feelings, her desires and her thoughts. Only as we wind up the conversation does she remember to ask, and how are you and the kids? This is just one example of many. Ultimately, everything begins and ends with her.

6) **Your mother is unable to show empathy.** When these daughters grow up, they are certain that their feelings don't matter. Moreover, they reject and repress their emotions. To this day, I have to ask myself how I feel about something. If I have a particularly strong response to something, I usually feel it in my stomach. It takes me a long time to understand the feeling, but now I allow myself to feel – something I hadn't done before. I repressed my feelings for many years so that my emotions wouldn't be a source of pain. It was much easier not to feel anything than to feel hurt.

7) **Your mother is unable to cope with her own emotions.** My mother blamed other people for everything. Our financial state was the fault of my unsuccessful father. If I asked her why she was so nasty to me, she claimed I was imagining it. I was distorting what had actually happened; she hadn't used the words I said she had used. In general, "my imagination" was something she often maligned. It was easier for her to tell me I was imagining things than to deal with my accusations.

8) **Your mother is critical and judgmental.** McBride writes that narcissistic adults have a hard time coming to terms with the fact that as children, they were treated critically and judgmentally. The reason narcissistic mothers are so critical is that they themselves lack self-confidence. They project their

frustration onto their daughters, blaming them for their unhappiness, making them feel that they aren't good enough. My mother repeatedly told me that she never loved my father and that she only stayed with him because she became pregnant one month after their wedding. I am the oldest child. (Obviously this has nothing to do with reality, but still…). My mother blamed my father for their finances, and frequently claimed that if she had married someone else, her life would have been much better.

9) **Your mother relates to you as a friend, not as a mother.** In a healthy mother-daughter relationship, the mother acts like a parent and looks after her daughter. The daughter should be taken care of by her mother, not the other way around. Narcissistic mothers need a mother because they didn't get the mothering they required. They switch roles: the daughters function as an audience, a source of attention, love and affection. In these families, it is the daughters who are supposed to give to their mothers. My mother always told my relatives that she and I were real "friends," that we went out for coffee together and talked about everything under the sun. (I never shared anything personal with my mother for a simple reason: I didn't want to give her more reasons for criticizing and complaining about me.) From a young age, my mother exposed me to information that was not appropriate for children, about my father and about other people. From the moment my children were born, I said to them – and I still say to them – that I am not their friend. They have plenty of friends, but only one mother. My job is to care about them and to care for them, not necessarily in the manner of a friend.

10) **There are no boundaries between you and your mother.** In terms of emotions, a narcissistic mother does not allow her

daughter to grow up and become a separate entity. The mother sees the daughter as an extension of herself. Narcissistic mothers experience many difficulties. They are extremely insecure, and they have a constant need for love and admiration. They see themselves as very important, and must be the center of attention everywhere, all the time. What is particularly harmful is their desire to eradicate the womanly part of their daughters, or anything else that can turn their daughters into competitors. The most narcissistic mothers will try to shatter their daughters' self-confidence in every possible way; they feel threatened when their daughters are growing and blossoming. In my case, I knew with absolute certainty that anything personal would be transmitted to the entire family, and so I could never share my troubles and my thoughts. As for my femininity, my mother gave me negative messages, and any feminine problems were never addressed, to the point of neglect. These complicated relationships are confusing to daughters of narcissistic mothers: it leads them to seek affirmation from anyone at hand, look for love where there isn't any, and get hurt time after time.

CHAPTER TWO
Conditional Love

What is love? How do we know when we love someone? How do we bestow love on others?

When I asked my mother what love was, she thought I was asking about falling in love. "Falling in love is when you have butterflies in your stomach." That's how she described love. The first time I fell in love, she told me she envied me, despite the fact that I had fallen for someone who didn't love me back. When my love was reciprocated, she didn't like it at all. When I went to live with my partner, my mother warned me, "He's just going to take advantage of you, then one day he'll throw you out and who's going to want you then?" Didn't she consider the possibility that the opposite might happen, that we'd live together happily for the rest of our lives? Or that I would choose to live with a different partner? I remember her exact words; they sharpened my sense that I was undeserving of love.

My partner and I lived together for a year in Tel Aviv, and I was continually begging my family to come for dinner. The one time my mother came with my father, she sat on the edge of her seat, as if she was afraid of getting contaminated. The following year, we lived in England. That year, my mother eagerly came to visit and even stayed with us in our crowded little apartment. And we weren't even married. She was much more concerned with what other people would say than with my happiness.

My mother didn't talk to me about love and friendship. I believed I wasn't worthy of love. She didn't really understand the concept of love. I never complained to her about this, since she was certain that she knew what love was, but her idea of love had nothing to do with true love. Because my mother is unable to see me as a separate person, she can't recognize anything that benefits me unless it benefits her as well. I couldn't understand how she could never think about me and my desires, but only about what would serve her best, and we argued about this frequently. Whenever my wishes were not aligned with hers, she behaved manipulatively or explosively or in some other inappropriate way. I found this quite frightening. As a child, I generally heeded her wishes, but as I grew up, I began to put my own wishes first, despite the heavy price that I had to pay.

There were long periods of time in which my mother refused to speak to me. Whenever I found a new close friend, my mother would warn me off, insisting that a person couldn't depend on friends, only on family. How lucky I was that I didn't listen to her. My friends are a significant part of my life.

An inability to love

My mother's demonstrations of love (or, more accurately, of pleasantness and positivity) were always contingent on something. I desperately wanted to be a good girl, a good student, smart and fastidious – and it didn't come easily. I had undiagnosed attention deficit disorder; I ended up diagnosing myself when my oldest son was diagnosed with a learning disability. My mother treated me with something resembling love only when she herself could take credit for my successes. She never told me that she loved me, and she never made me feel that I succeeded at anything. When I gave birth to my third son, there was a complication with the caesarian delivery, and my recovery was long and painful. My mother kept repeating the same sentence, with a smile on her face: my son, she said, "was worth every tear." These words sicken me to this day. Of course my son is a treasure, worth any amount of pain, but I am her daughter. What kind of sentence is this to say to your daughter when she is suffering? A sentence that offers your daughter as a sacrifice.

When I got my master's degree in geography, I was already the mother of three children. I invited my mother to my graduation. When she got there and saw that I wasn't on the list of honor students, she asked angrily why I wasn't graduating with honors (she must have been disappointed that she couldn't brag about me to her friends, not that she had a problem with lying). When I received my master's in Hebrew literature, my mother sat in the audience and didn't stop interrupting me.

When she came to my wedding, my mother was, in her words, "stoned," having taken several tranquilizers. I was supposed to be the center of everything, not her. She managed to put herself at the center by demonstrating her misery to the extended family. I will never forget my wedding day. After all, it is one of the most meaningful and joyful days in a young woman's life. I woke up and went to my uncle and aunt's house, where the wedding would be, and made my own flower arrangements. (My future husband was going about his own business, as we had decided to spend the day apart.) When I finished taking care of the flowers, I went to the hair stylist by myself, then to my parents' house, where a family friend made up the faces of all the women.

Then we went to the wedding. Nobody uttered a word of pride or excitement. This was my wedding, my special day, not hers. How sad. When I look back on that day, what really shocks me is the fact that I didn't feel lonely, and that I didn't need anyone to spend the day with me, to prepare me for the ceremony, to pamper, love, and support me. The sad fact that I didn't even think I deserved someone like this appalls me. I can't even imagine that when my sons stand under the wedding canopy, I wouldn't try to rejoice with them, to give their desires their full weight.

A burdensome inheritance – my love for myself is also conditional

Because my mother's love for me was conditional, it wasn't really love. This is a painful realization. I had the good fortune to know that my father loved me unconditionally. He never came out and told me or my siblings that he loved us – he was a man of few words – but I knew that he gave of himself purely, not for his own personal gain. Looking back with the wisdom I've acquired over the years, I think that even now I don't really know how to "translate" people's behavior to me. Of course I have moments of closeness with people, but in general, these moments are accompanied by the unhealthy thought that they must want something from me.

It takes a long time before I feel that I can trust someone who loves me; from time to time, I still find myself wondering what these people see in me. Even my love for myself is, it seems, conditional. Bad habits are hard to break. Every day, through positive self-talk, I try to convince myself that I am indeed worthy of unconditional love, pure love like my father's. This is my way of trying to change this problematic equation.

CHAPTER THREE
Coping Mechanisms for Children of Narcissistic Moms

If I am not for myself, who will be?

Daughters of narcissistic mothers have different ways of coping. Some turn to narcotics and other drugs, others struggle with chronic depression. Those who choose not to put up a fight fall down and get consumed. I fought like a lion, always, in every situation, whether or not it was warranted. I argued all the time, stood up to her, proved her wrong when she lied. I made a clear distinction between her and me, and ultimately I did as I pleased. I paid a heavy price for all this.

From a very young age, I had what my mother called "nervous habits." She didn't understand why I was such a "nervous," "unsettled," and "rebellious" girl. (It's a good thing I was rebellious; if it had been up to her, I would have been her personal servant, hiding under her apron.)

My body reflected my distress. It expressed the emotions I couldn't articulate. I bit my fingernails, I fidgeted, I couldn't stay in my seat. All my mother did was tell me to stop; she never paused to think that there might have been a good reason for my behavior.

She was completely unpredictable. She could hug you one minute, then slap you the next. She could throw shoes at us or shatter dishes on the floor. Once she threw an iron at me; I don't remember what I had said. Maybe I really had been fresh. I remember running away. I walked all the way from our house in Herzliya to my aunt's house in Ramat HaSharon, a distance of several miles. For three days, I refused to go back home. I think I was about seventeen at the time. What amazes me to this day is the fact that anyone looking at us from the outside would have had no idea what was going on within our four walls. My mother always looked attractive and put-together; she was friendly and pleasant. It is easy to hide what really goes on behind someone's door.

My father was weak; I couldn't count on him for anything. The extended family would never have guessed; they saw what they wanted to see, and what people see can be very different than what's actually happening. Daughters of narcissistic mothers understand from a young age that they are alone. That if they won't pick themselves up, nobody else will. It pains me to compare the way I was as a young girl with the way I am as a mother. I always have my children's backs, and they know it.

As children, we think our families are just like other families. Children can't distinguish between different types of families. They have to find a way to deal with the reality into which they've been born. A child of a narcissistic mother doesn't understand that the family is in disrepair.

Without understanding why, I always knew I had to rely on myself, to keep my distance from the problems and to focus on what I really wanted. When something mattered to me, I would do everything in my power to get my way. I wasn't a wild or mean girl, but I insisted on doing things my way, even if my parents objected. All of this came at a cost, in stress and in a poor sense of self. However, it also gave me inner strength, because I knew then and I know now that although I may occasionally break, I can always put myself back together and move on. Children of narcissistic mothers are simply trying to survive in difficult circumstances. They have no choice. Either they are swallowed up or they fight back. I chose to fight back.

Body image – You have to do something about your body...

And it was my body, this body that bothered her so much. It wasn't thin enough, it developed too early, my eyes were the wrong color, I was the wrong height, and my breasts were much too big.

"You have to do something about your body…." This is the sentence I heard my mother say every time we went shopping for clothes. "You can't go on like this, you have to do something about your body." Sometimes it was, "You take after your father's family, not me. You got your fat legs from your aunts." What was she thinking when she said those kinds of things? She never told me I was pretty. She never told me I was wonderful, or even good enough. She never said anything positive about me. She only talked about what I did or didn't do, not about who I really was. And even if I had what she thought of as "the right body," would she have been supportive? The answer is clear. There was no connection between my appearance and the messages my mother gave me about my body.

Body image is a complicated issue for all girls, but it's especially challenging for daughters of narcissistic mothers. Daughters like us didn't get the attention, encouragement and acceptance that we needed. We never heard a kind word. The subject of body image is particularly fraught. I went through periods of starving myself to look "sexy," and my mother didn't say a word. There were also times when I ate endlessly in an effort to quash my emotional pain.

Narcissistic mothers, like the evil queen in Snow White, are horrified when their daughters turn into young women. Watching their daughters' budding femininity is very hard for them. They compete with their daughters, and will do their best to suppress their development. "It's impossible with your body." "You have to do something about your body." I heard these sentences regularly. (My sister didn't "merit" this gift; she "merited" other gifts pertaining to her intelligence.) As a girl, I didn't like my body. I tried to hide it with oversize clothes that blurred the lines of my figure, but that didn't please my mother, either. She reprimanded me for wearing "rags." I remember fighting with her constantly about what to wear to events. These wars were accompanied by humiliation and hurt feelings. I came to the conclusion that no matter what I did, there was something wrong with me.

At the age of fourteen, I started going to Weight Watchers. I remember enrolling by myself (at my mother's encouragement), and attending meetings by myself. I look at photographs from that period, and I can't fathom why I went. I wasn't emaciated, but I wasn't overweight, either. My mother decided she was going to "help me lose weight." She prepared low-calorie salads for me, alongside the meat patties and other foods that she made for everyone else – those who weren't watching their weight.

Problems with body image have plagued me for as long as I can remember. In the diary I kept as a ten-year old fourth-grader, I wrote that "I started a grapefruit juice diet." I read this, and I am appalled by the messages I was receiving. My mother herself suffers from eating disorders. When I was young, she tried to teach me how to make myself throw up (and I later discovered she had secretly tried to teach my son as well). After a large meal, she would announce that she was going "to stick a finger" because she had eaten too much. A few years ago, when my oldest son told me that she had tried to teach him this technique, too, I was shocked to the depths of my soul. I am incredulous that my issues with body image aren't even more severe.

My mother puts a lot of stock in appearance. She always looks "just so," and she talks about the men who compliment her on her youthful appearance, her lovely eyes. The skin is more important that what's beneath it.

Why do narcissistic mothers transmit such unhealthy messages to their daughters?

In her article "Daughters of Narcissistic Mothers – a Legacy of Psychological Pain,"[3] Dr. Linda Martinez-Lewi discusses the body image of these daughters. She argues that jealousy is the driving force in these mother-daughter relationships. Jealousy all the time, in every situation. Things take a turn for the worse when the daughters start to turn into women. Because the mother feels like

---

[3] Freeing Yourself from the Narcissist in Your Life, Dr. Linda Martinez-Lewi (2013)

she is competing with her daughter, she tries to hijack her daughter's femininity in any way possible.

Do I have a healthy body image today? The answer isn't simple. The issue of weight continues to be my constant companion. I try to compliment my children, to bolster their confidence in their external and internal attractiveness, but as a role model, I'm afraid they see a mother who is always struggling with her weight. It is very hard to break away from the place you've come from.

I believe that being aware of the issue, and focusing on health rather than on weight and body image, is helpful. At this point in my life, my physical and emotional health are very important to me.

I recognize that in all likelihood, I will always struggle with this issue, but what is different now is my acceptance of myself as I am, with no self-loathing. Weight is just weight, and weighing more or less will not make me happier or unhappier, only healthier or unhealthier.

My weight does not determine who I am, and it is important for me to love myself regardless of my size. What has changed over the years is that I finally accept and love myself. I have a mantra which I repeat regularly, an affirmation of something that doesn't come naturally to me: "I am deserving. I am good enough. I deserve love."

THE COST OF SHAME

Feeling like an alien species

Nobody in this world has the right to control other people, to humiliate, insult, hurt and especially shame them. I think shame was the primary emotion I felt as a girl. I was ashamed of my body, of the way I talked, of my weakness, of my failures, of the fact that I was never good enough. I was ashamed of myself and ashamed of my parents and siblings. I never felt like I belonged; I always felt like an alien species. I believe that my family saw me that way, too.

Shame is a feeling that can wash over me without warning. Shame of who I am, of my mother, of the fact that even now I don't always feel worthy. These are things I've experienced from a young age. Shame helps the controller maintain control. It is very hard to free oneself from shame, and it has been with me for all my fifty years. I wonder if other women feel this way.

Screaming to be heard: finding my voice

When my parents moved from an apartment in Ramat Gan to a house in Herzliya, something significant took place. I was fourteen, and I was anxious about the move, just as any girl would be. My aunt, who lived in Ramat HaSharon, told me once that I would have to change the way I spoke, because people in Herzliya speak differently. Because of this conversation, I was scared to talk for an entire year, even when the twin girls in my class were bullying me on a daily basis. Once, the school took us to a performance at a theater in Tel Aviv. I don't remember exactly what the girls said to me, but I remember crying the whole way home. When I got to my house and my mother saw me crying, she was sure I had been raped. Petrified, she asked me what happened; I don't remember how she reacted when I told her.

I do know, however, that she didn't take any action: she didn't talk to anyone at the school, she didn't call the girl's parents. As usual, I had to cope with this by myself. One day, I decided to spend recess in the classroom, and the girls started to bother me again. I remember screaming – a scream that was disproportionate to the situation. The girls were so scared, they didn't speak to me for the rest of high school.

I understood that if I didn't have a voice, I wouldn't have anything. Regrettably, my listeners didn't always appreciate my strongly-voiced opinions. As a girl, I had claimed the role of "defender of freedom and social justice – revealer of the truth." When I think back to my childhood and the role I adopted, I realize that I was always trying to find the truth amid all the secrets and lies, to dig it out from the pile of hollow words, hoping that by discovering the truth I would understand how I fit into my family. I think that's why I either remained silent or shouted – because I couldn't find my voice.

Even before that, I had come to realize that if I didn't defend myself, nobody else would. One of the problems faced by daughters of narcissistic mothers is that they give up before the battle even starts. **They don't dare make a sound.** They don't ask for help because they know there's nobody to ask. Even now, when I'm struggling, I don't ask for help; I withdraw into myself. Fortunately, I have a partner who knows how to reach out his hand and pull me out of my shell. **Being a girl without a voice had grave results,** including poor self-image and an inability to rely on other people or to put my trust in them. This created an internal conflict, in which I had to choose between fighting and disappearing. Later, this conflict led me to rebel. I am rebellious and opinionated when I have to be, and also when I don't.

CHAPTER FOUR
The Dual Nature of Imagination

The power of imagination

Like many young girls, I loved to play make-believe. I liked to read books about girls who were loved and mothers who were protective, about loving and protective fathers, even about naughty girls whose mothers loved them despite their bad behavior. I imagined a future in which I'd be married to someone who loved me, and we'd have adorable children whom I would love and who would love me back.

Imagination was my refuge when things were painful and difficult. After playing out these imaginary scenarios, the world seemed much brighter, and I could return to the real-world ready to cope with every-day life. During my adolescence, imagination helped me create the life I yearned for.

Imagination is a wonderful tool that I continue to use today: when I'm writing, when I'm enjoying something, when I'm not getting along with someone. It is a unique and wondrous device. All of us can call upon our imagination. When I say that imagination is something I use, I'm talking about guided imagination. I used this tool as a child without realizing that it was an established therapeutic technique, and over the years imagination has afforded me some relief from hardship, pain, emotional neglect and abuse. Imagination is a safe haven for all of us. Nobody in this world can enter our minds and read our thoughts. For me, imagination was a personal space that my mother couldn't infiltrate; it was mine alone.

Even today, after the long journey I have taken (and am still taking), my imagination helps me heal. Karyl McBride – herself the daughter of a narcissistic mother – shares one example of how she used imagination as part of her therapeutic process. McBride bought a doll and imagined that it was the little girl she had been. She sat with the doll for a long time, feeling things, empowering herself, essentially behaving – on a small scale – the way a loving and encouraging mother would behave with her daughter. She and I both had mothers who couldn't do this for us.

With the help of the imagination, people can heal the parts of themselves that are in pain. And eventually, after grieving for the childhood they never had, after acceptance and forgiveness, it is much easier to move on.

Imagination as a tool for healing

I had an active imagination that took me to all sorts of happy and beautiful places where everyone was polite and loving, where people hugged and kissed and didn't yell. A peaceful and predictable place, where outrageous things didn't happen every five minutes. In my imaginary world, fathers behaved like fathers, mothers like mothers. Mothers loved their daughters, worried about them, caressed them and supported them.

I first discovered this world in books, then later in movies. Feelings of warmth, pleasure and security enveloped me when I read or played make-believe with my neighborhood friends or my cousins. At those times, the world really would be safe and good. I loved songs, and I loved singing. Every day I would listen to the radio show "For Mother and Child," which aired from 2-4 pm. I would do my homework while listening to stories and conversations, and my world would become calm and pleasant.

Imagination isn't just a means of survival or disparagement, as I discuss in the next section; it is also a means of repair, of asking forgiveness and of forgiving. I forgave my mother. I forgave her, but that doesn't mean I don't continue to be cautious. As long as she is alive, I will be careful when we communicate. The fact that I didn't have a protective mother is much less painful for me now than it used to be, and I can now understand that she had her own troubles, and forgive her.

Imagination is an enormous gift. It encompasses absolute freedom. I can share things that come into my imagination, or I can choose not to share them. In our imagination, we can go wherever we please, be whoever we want to be, take care of things any way we like. We're free.

My mother had no access to my imagination, and so it was the only place I was free to do as I pleased without her taking control. Imagination healed my heart, and allowed me to think about a different path and a different life. Even now, I sometimes use my imagination to calm myself down when things are difficult. Happily, I use it a lot less than I did as a child, for the simple reason that I no longer need it as much.

Ultimately, imagination led me to be a writer. Writing has accompanied me like an old friend since I picked up a pencil, but as a child, it never occurred to me that one day I would write books, lecture around the world, and support budding authors. I have always written poems and stories, but becoming a professional writer was a long process that grew out of my passion for justice.

"Daughter of Iraq," my first book, seeks to revisit the decades-old literary and social depiction of Iraqi women as weak and degraded. The book took me five years to write, and won a prize from the Babylonian Jewish Heritage Center (Babylon is now Iraq). From that point on, I realized that this was my mission; it was the career I had spent so many years looking for. Now I do everything I can to support young writers, as well as other daughters of narcissistic mothers. The very thing that saved me during my childhood became a creative power and a professional path.

Imagination as a means of disparagement and humiliation

The sentence "It's just your imagination" hurts me to this day. My mother used it to taunt me. Her words made me feel belittled. They also wreaked havoc with my emotions and my memories – did it really happen the way I remembered it, or did I actually imagine it, as my mother claimed?

Whenever I leveled an accusation at my mother, she shook it off immediately. Her preferred response was to mock me: It was "just my imagination" – it never actually happened. She used this sentence regularly; apparently, she couldn't accept guilt or blame. Every time she thrust this sentence at me, I set out to prove myself right, thereby earning a reputation as my family's "justice fighter." When I say "my family," I mean my extended family. They didn't understand that the fact that I was so often accused of "imagining things" was what led me to question reality and to investigate whether something had or hadn't really happened.

Whenever I was certain that it wasn't my imagination, that something had in fact happened the way I remembered it, I declared all-out war. It didn't matter what the issue was – perhaps I was defending my right to do something, or maybe someone had put me down – but regardless, I needed to prove that the episode happened, that it was the truth, that my feelings were justified.

It was much simpler for my mother to argue that I was imagining things than to face the truth, but it was very harmful to me. When someone tells a young girl that what she sees or hears is all in her imagination, she begins to wonder if her wise mother knows something she doesn't know. If her mother says she's imagining it, maybe she really is.

And if you can imagine an event, maybe your emotions aren't credible either. Maybe if you're sad or angry or hurt, that, too, is all in your imagination. If that's the case, the only solution is to suppress your feelings so that you don't feel anything at all. If you neglect or conceal your feelings, nobody can tell you that you're "imagining things. If you hide your feelings, nothing hurts, the waters are placid, your mother isn't angry, and you no longer care what's true and what isn't. You stop trusting yourself, and even worse, you stop trusting your feelings, which can cause tremendous emotional damage.

Sometimes I am beset by feelings that seem to come out of nowhere. I used to wait for these emotions to run their course; I didn't understand where they came from, and I was ashamed of their intensity. Now, I pause for a minute. I try to figure out what I'm feeling; I breathe, I breathe again. I look for the source of the emotion. Most of the time I find it, and I feel a huge sense of relief. The suppression of emotions is a chronic struggle for the daughters of narcissistic mothers.

As I write this, I am choking up and my heart is pounding – it's an automatic response. My response used to be to fight. I fought tirelessly for the truth, even for my sanity; after all, it would have been so easy to fall into the hole that my mother had dug for me, to turn into her prisoner. Some inner power compelled me to fight, and as it turned out, it was this power that saved me.

CHAPTER FIVE
The Cost of Childhood Neglect

How did I raise myself?

My mother was not able to deal with me, or to help me. She was focused on her own life, and was unable to understand the problems I encountered at every stage of my childhood. I think her primary problem was her inability to pay attention to anyone else's needs. Now, after going through the therapy process and reading McBride's book, I have no grievances with her. She did the best she could. But "the best she could" was deeply hurtful. From a very young age, I understood that I was responsible for my own fate, that if I didn't take care of myself, nobody would. Many times I fell into deep despair. I remember several quintessential moments when I didn't even expect help. (Needless to say, I didn't get it. In fact, quite the opposite.)

I tried to minimize my hardships, not to talk about them too much, because every difficulty I faced provided my mother with an opportunity to taunt me, to hurt me, to prove that I didn't deserve to be listened to. It is painful to admit this, but her only aspiration was complete control. When I was a nineteen-year old soldier, I was head over heels in love with someone who didn't love me back. I was in the army's Nachal unit at the time, and he and I were in the same cohort. My mother hadn't wanted me to join Nachal in the first place; she wanted me to stay at her side, and did everything she could to persuade me to leave the army and go home. I remember falling into dark pits of despondency, but I held on by the skin of my teeth: I didn't give up, and I finished my service. This came at a large emotional cost – intense disappointment, which I took as confirmation that I didn't deserve to be loved – but it also showed me that I was stronger than I thought, and that I could extricate myself from difficult situations.

It is hard for me to understand her behavior, and even harder for me to accept, especially now, when I myself am the mother of adolescent boys, and their welfare supersedes everything else. As I write, I think about the little girl inside me. Was I truly unworthy of a listening ear, support, empathy, and understanding?

I have lived with emotional neglect and physical abuse since I was very young. When my mother got angry at me, she used to throw me down on the floor. She'd yell at me that she wasn't my mother anymore, that I should go away. She did the same to my siblings. When I was only nine years old and just starting fourth grade, I went through a period of time when I was essentially excommunicated: it was as if I wasn't even there. I don't remember if I told her about it; by then I understood that I was alone.

When I was disappointed in my friends, she told me that I couldn't count on friends. When I had trouble with teachers, she didn't do anything. When people spoke to me crudely or insulted me, she joined them in their mockery. When I didn't do what she wanted me to do, she stopped talking to me.

Whenever my inclinations were different than hers, she went out of her way to turn the whole family against me. To my chagrin, that pattern continues to this day, even though she is now eighty-two and I am fifty. She never accepted me, and she never respected my choices, opinions, or thoughts. From a young age, I understood that there was nobody to protect me, so I had to protect myself. I was a freedom fighter and a rebel, and I stood my ground despite her antagonism.

Girls who are used to standing alone and protecting themselves do not expect much from the world. They understand that they are solely responsible for their lives. Those who don't break become stronger and more independent, and those who do break – well, their entire lives break as well. These children learn to put their feelings to sleep, whatever those feelings may be, to avoid getting hurt. Some of them do this through various addictions – to food, to drugs, to sex. I had my own unusual ways of numbing the pain. Involuntary tics, frequent explosive fits of rage. I learned to suppress my feelings, to push them away – if they weren't there, they couldn't hurt me. And I could always escape to my room, to its music or its silence. All I wanted was to be left alone. In addition, I was very lucky: I could have deteriorated (and to some extent, when I was in an emotional abyss, I did), but I was resourceful, and I had a loving and encouraging partner. I understood that I had to take myself in hand. I think that if I hadn't realized that, I would not be here today. Yes, that's how bad it was.

To this day, when people talk to me disrespectfully, I am stunned by their nerve and power, but I don't know how to stop them. My anger only rears its head after the episode is over. I am angry at myself for not being able to stop people from mistreating me. I allow people to behave badly again and again, falling back into my role as a helpless little girl. I understand this, but deep down, I don't feel it. This gap – between what I know and what I feel – has been an integral part of myself throughout my entire life.

In addition to emotional neglect, there was physical neglect – and abuse – as well. It wasn't something that the outside world could see. Narcissistic mothers make a point of putting up a good front. Their children are always wearing clean clothes. My teeth were straightened (even though I had to take a bus, by myself, to another city to do so. I was eleven at the time, and I had begged my mother not to make me do it). I had hormonal problems starting at age twelve, when I got my period for the first time. I used to faint on the first day of my period. My mother didn't think of taking me to the doctor. All my "nervous habits" elicited no response other than nasty comments and derisive laughter. But I did get new clothes. After all, I had to look well-dressed and well-groomed. Beyond that, I didn't get much.

When people talk about emotional neglect, they don't mean that they're simply not being heard; they mean that their feelings are ignored, even nullified. Their emotions are treated as irrelevant and unimportant. Successes and accomplishments don't matter, unless of course the mother can claim them for herself. These children grow up believing that their emotions, whatever they may be, are irrelevant. Girls like me cope with this by numbing their feelings or by believing that they are unworthy.

To a certain extent, there was emotional abuse as well. When someone dismisses your feelings, it is abuse. When someone mocks your feelings, it is abuse. When you are taught that your feelings are unimportant or irrelevant – that, too, is abuse. My mother frequently compared me to my cousins, asking why I wasn't more like them.

There was no room for who I actually was, there was no respect, and there was, essentially, no love.

CHAPTER SIX
The Role of the Fathers

The leading actress and the supporting actor

My father was the first male figure in my life. In my eyes, he was weak, too weak to help me, particularly when it came to his ability to explain things to me. My father was so overshadowed by my mother that he barely existed. It's true, I grew up at a time when fathers were less involved in their children's lives, but my father was absent more than he was present.

My father supported the family and did the cooking, but that was the extent of his involvement in our lives. He was a good man, but he didn't function as a real father. Aside from matters relating to food and driving, perhaps occasionally politics, we didn't talk. He was extremely right-wing, and we would argue about political issues. I didn't seek his advice; I didn't see him as the kind of man who could guide me wisely. Besides, because he was such a quiet man, we had never become accustomed to talking to him. Although my father didn't always show it, I knew that he loved me. He didn't say much, but I always knew that if I needed him, he would be there for me. That's what people mean when they talk about "unconditional love."

My father was a man of peace. He may have straggled behind my mother, but he never spoke to me, or about me, with disrespect. He helped me whenever I asked him to, without asking questions. It's hard to explain how I knew that he would always be there for me, but I knew. I didn't feel like I had to do anything special for him to love and accept me as I was; it was clear to me that he already did. Still, he was always engrossed in his own business and wasn't interested in our day-to-day activities, our hobbies, or anything else. I think the fact that he didn't criticize or bother me gave me a sense of serenity and security.

I learned from the articles I read that the husbands of narcissistic women tend to be meek and inconspicuous, and in this respect my father fit the bill. He admired and adored my mother. Now, as a mother myself, I think about him and try to remember if he ever argued with her about our education; I don't think he did. Our education was my mother's domain, since anything related to our public lives was of the utmost importance to her. My father gave her the widest berth possible. He never envied her, he just stood by her and supported her.

The only things they would argue about were finances and cooking; on all other matters, my father never stood his ground. My mother was never content with our financial state, no matter how much money we had. There was nothing my father could do. This was the constant state of affairs, which was one of the things that led me to promise myself I would never be like her.

My father was, in fact, an excellent cook. I don't know many Iraqi men who could cook like he did. He baked desserts, too, but what he really excelled in was traditional Iraqi main dishes. Everything he prepared came out well. To this day, everyone who has ever eaten his food talks about it with a wistful look in their eyes.

My attitude towards him is complicated. On the one hand, I love him, I remember him fondly, and I understand that he did everything he could; on the other hand, I am also angry at him. Where was he? Why didn't he help me when I was a little girl? Why was he always so distant? Why didn't he support me? Why didn't he go to parent-teacher conferences? Why didn't he come to my parties? While my mother paid my father no heed, she always welcomed the input of her two brothers, who also served as father figures for me. I remember my uncle going to parent-teacher meetings – didn't I find that strange? My father owned a store, but he could have found someone to cover for him if he wanted to leave for a few hours. I know that was another era, and men were less involved in their children's lives, but there's a difference between being there occasionally and not being there at all.

My father worked from morning until noon; then he would come home to eat lunch and rest. He would return to the store at four, then come back home at about eight in the evening. He was home for several hours every day, but all I remember is the meal and the rest, not even a greeting when he came home. We'd shout, "Hi, Dad, come say hello!" and he might peek his head in and say a quick hello, but that was it. When he came back in the evening, he would often cook for the next day or watch TV with us. I don't remember having meaningful discussions with him. My father had no idea what grade we were in; we would test him, then burst out laughing, because he always got things wrong. He kept out of things.

When he got old and sick, he became more invested in his grandchildren. He spent hours pushing them on the swing outside our house. He cooked for us, went shopping with me, and walked around our neighborhood. My father was a man of actions, not words, and when we were little, he wasn't interested in our problems or our conflicts with our mother. We were clean and we had food on our plates, and that was enough for him.

My father died from lung cancer about eight years ago. In the last week of his life, he visited us in our house in Tel Aviv. He had his special armchair in my garden, and a red leather sofa in the living room that he liked to rest on. That sofa is still in my office to this day. Sometimes I use it to rest, other times to think.

The last time he came to visit us (and left in an ambulance because he was having trouble breathing), I made kebabs. My father loved kebabs. I put a small one on his plate and sat next to him. My father looked at it, then at me, then at the kebab again. "I can't eat," he said, "but don't tell Mom."

I will never forget that sentence. My father, who was dying, thought not about himself but about my mother. He didn't want to make her angry or sad. She could tend to him and be angry with him at the same time. A strange but interesting combination.

In the final hours of his life, my father wanted to tell me about something that had happened a long time ago, something that had to do with me. With tears in his eyes, he told me that once, after I moved out of their house, he drove me to the apartment I shared with my partner. At the time, my parents were strapped for money. "I told you," he said, "that I had cash on me, and I offered you as much as you wanted. I knew you were supporting yourself and paying your own tuition; I knew things were hard for you. At first, you refused, then you agreed to accept only fifty shekels. You left me drowning in my tears." I didn't remember this episode, but I clearly knew that I could rely on myself, and I didn't want to be a burden to my parents.

When a patient asks the empty chair – on which her father theoretically sits – "Dad, where were you? Why didn't you protect me?", there is no answer. In her book, McBride writes, "Father is revolving around Mother like a planet around the sun."[4] She explains that narcissistic women choose partners who will allow them to be at the center of every situation; if the partner won't play that role, the marriage can't survive.

In the family drama, the narcissistic woman is the star, her partner the supporting actor. In the peculiar relationship between my parents, I saw my mother as the lead, while my father stepped out of the spotlight and worshiped the ground she walked on.

My mother told me many times that she married him because "he was the peskiest" of all her suitors, and because he had an apartment near her sister and brother-in-law. She added, "I got married to put an end to all the bad things people were saying about me." (Of course, she never talked about the fact that she didn't get married until the age of thirty-one, which in those days was considered very old; she didn't want people to know how old she

---

[4] Will I ever be Free, Karyl McBride, page 60.

was.) "I decided," she said, "that I would get a divorce one month after my wedding, but I became pregnant and so I stayed." This was like saying to me, her oldest daughter, "It's all your fault!" She "pitied him," and made sure to tell him on a regular basis that "she never loved him." I remember how hurt I felt on his behalf, and to a certain extent I tried to compensate for her lack of love. As a child, I loved him and admired him, and when I grew up, I loved him and ached for him.

CHAPTER SEVEN
All That Glitters... The Gap Between Appearance and Reality

From the day my mother gave birth to me, she's enjoyed talking about "her" pregnancy: how she felt, how she couldn't wait for the baby to be born. When I was three months old, she went back to work. She said she continued to breast-feed me "so she wouldn't get pregnant." Even her breastfeeding had a purpose that had nothing to do with me. A year later, my mother got pregnant again, and gave birth to my brother. She continued to work, hiring a "walker" to take us outside when she got home, so she could rest. All told, she spent very little time with us. A few years later my sister was born, at which point my mother left her job and stayed home with us.

There was always a hot meal waiting for us when we got home, that much I can say. We were well-dressed, and from the outside, everything looked fine. We usually spent the afternoons at our cousin's houses. My mother liked to visit them, and we would go with her whether we wanted to or not. On weekends, we visited my grandparents and other relatives. Sometimes it was wonderful and sometimes they heaped criticism on me. I don't remember why; I must have been disrespectful. Their criticism made me defensive; after all, if nobody else was going to advocate for me, I had to advocate for myself.

How much can you tell about a family from the outside? Nothing! All you can do is get an impression, and a superficial one at that. What actually goes on inside the house is known only to its inhabitants. Narcissistic mothers know how to hide their family's flaws. For these mothers, looking wonderful and putting on a good show are critical. I think this is one of the reasons I still have trouble accepting compliments on my mothering skills from anyone who doesn't live in my house. The view from out there isn't the same as the view from in here. These people have no idea what happens inside my home; they never see me in challenging, complicated situations, or in moments of sadness and anger. There's no way for them to judge how I treat my children when things aren't going smoothly.

The big question is, how does a woman who grew up with a narcissistic mother construct a different kind of motherhood – a motherhood that is not narcissistic? There's no simple answer. The luckier daughters understood what was going on and were able to take care of themselves. The less fortunate ones understood only that something was not right. These daughters often felt lost and confused; some imitated the model they grew up with, others tried their best to change things, but none of them ever felt "good enough."

PART TWO
HOW DID I AVOID TURNING INTO MY MOTHER?

CHAPTER EIGHT
Choosing a Life Partner – Who Would Love Me, Anyway?

For daughters of narcissistic mothers, choosing a life partner is complicated and challenging. They often seek out men who embody their mother's characteristics, or, alternatively, look for idealized versions of their father. These relationships often fail. In my case, during my teenage years and the years immediately following, I fell in love with people who didn't love me back. ([I was also involved with people who did love me back, but those people didn't interest me in the least.) In my eyes, the unrequited love I experienced was a replication of the rejection I'd felt as a child. The more the object of my love didn't love me back, the more "at home" I felt: undeserving of love, not good enough, not feminine enough, not sexy.... In other words, I felt like a failure, and not feeling loved was the emotion I was most familiar with from the day I was born.

I don't know how I managed to fall in love with a man who loved me back so fiercely. We got married and had four sons, and together we are raising our family with tremendous love. I believe that this reciprocal love was nothing short of a miracle, and to this day, after nearly thirty years of sharing a life with this man, I still see my requited love as a miracle. It is not something I would ever take for granted.

My partner and I have come a long way in our relationship,

which wasn't always easy. We overcame many crises and hardships. In our case, mutual love triumphed over (and continues to triumph over) our everyday demons. The secret of our successful marriage is awareness and the ability to address problems as they arise.

As a young woman, I wasn't cognizant of the real reason I fell in love with my spouse – feeling loved, feeling comfortable in my own skin. I was in love, my partner loved me back (unlike in my previous relationships), and after three years of living together, we got married. While our love for each other was strong, our desire to better ourselves, to grow both as a couple and as individuals, was no less strong. If this hadn't been the case, our marriage would not have survived. Every crisis led to growth, and every hardship taught us something about ourselves and our marriage. Yes, there were moments of desolation, even of despair, but there was also the resolve to mend the rifts, to grow from them, to carry on.

In her book, Karyl McBride argues that for daughters of narcissistic mothers, partnership is complicated. They can never feel truly loved or deserving. I can imagine how exhausting it must be to be married to a woman who never feels worthy of love.

McBride emphasizes that women will try to find love, or something that looks like love, in a wide range of places. Often, they end up in exploitative or abusive relationships; they can't break the cycle, and so their marriages don't survive. Some women are unable to overcome the difficulties; they can't stop themselves from replicating the absence of maternal love through the absence of spousal love. Frequently, daughters of narcissistic mothers marry people who remind them of their mothers, thus reconstructing the absence of love. They yearn for love but are unable to attain intimacy.

Sometimes they marry men who belittle them, who don't appreciate them; they see nothing wrong with this. After all, that's what feels most familiar to them. They seek men who don't really desire them, then fight endlessly for a love that can never be actualized. Similarly, they have unrealistic expectations from their husbands, which also destine them to failure. There is nobody in the world who can sustain those kinds of demands. Being aware, says McBride, can improve the situation.

McBride claims that daughters of narcissistic mothers often construct relationships in which they are either the givers or the recipients of care. There is no balance of power. The question is always going to be either "What will I get out of it?" or "What will he get out of it?" In both cases, the love is not authentic; it is contingent upon the circumstances. The partners' need for love is not fulfilled, because the love is conditional.

In both of the above scenarios, the daughters feel that they have "come home," that they have returned to the place that is most familiar to them. They hope that in exchange for fulfilling someone else's needs, they will be worthy of appreciation and love. But in relationships like these, the other partner is usually looking for nothing more than a caretaker. And the reverse is true, too. In exchange for everything they do for their wives, the husbands receive something that looks like love, but bears no resemblance to true love. These unfortunate women never get to experience love.

Another option is to give up on the whole idea of marriage. These women, who don't feel deserving of love, give up at the outset. They build an independent life for themselves, a life that doesn't depend on anyone else. In the process, they lose out on a lot. They never experience marital love and partnership, and many of them never experience motherhood.

One of my greatest challenges, for example, is accepting criticism. I've never met anyone who likes being criticized, but it's especially hard for me. When someone criticizes me, I feel as if I've been stabbed with a knife. I've learned to take deep breaths, and I now understand that the criticism doesn't define me, doesn't make me less of a person. Its purpose is to make things better. The reason I respond the way I do is that whenever I did something that my mother didn't approve of, I knew I was in danger – of obliteration. If I wasn't acceptable, I was taught, I did not exist. I was not loved. I was rejected. This thought weighs heavily upon my soul. For many years, my husband has had a hard time criticizing any of my actions because I have so little toleration for it. Either I get vehemently defensive, or I go on the offensive, as if my life were in jeopardy. The criticism never feels like it pertains to a specific action, but to my entire being. Dealing with criticism was, and continues to be, hard for me, and it is an ongoing struggle in our marriage.

At the same time, awareness and therapy can help us choose the right partner. The sooner, and the better, we take care of ourselves, the more successful we will be at building healthy and positive relationships, which in turn accelerate the healing process. The greater our awareness and understanding, the more likely we are to create honest and loving marital relationships.

CHAPTER NINE
Friendships and Other Non-Marital Relationships

How we choose our friends over the years is no less fascinating than how we choose our spouses. I find it interesting to look back and think about which of my early friendships lasted until today and which didn't; which friendships fundamentally changed and which didn't. What kind of friends did I look for when I was younger? Which relationships survived and which didn't?

During my teenage years, my closest friendships were "unrealized" – they were close and not close at the same time. I think I invested much more in these friendships than the others did. I remember feeling tremendous frustration, but also deep closeness. A more accurate explanation for this phenomenon is, I believe, that although I didn't feel worthy of my friends' love, I fought for it tirelessly. It was just like what I experienced at home, although my teenage struggle for my mother's love was accompanied by my rejection of her behavior, a duality that lasted long into my adulthood.

Over the years, I found myself involved in a different kind of relationship, too: friendships that were disagreeable, full of drama. Friendships that were hard for me to be a part of. I was often drawn into friendships with dominant women who didn't leave much room for me. Today, to my delight and good fortune, my friendships are very different. The older I get, the more I find myself in loving and caring relationships that support me and accept me as I am. Today, I have close friends who are loving and beloved; we have been close for decades. Despite the physical distance between us, these relationships are close and inclusive, marked by allowing each other both space and respect. I was lucky. I imagine that for most people, the nature of friendship changes over the years, but for daughters of narcissistic mothers, the changes are profound. The contrast between "before" and "after" is striking. Awareness makes all the difference.

And still, my biggest stumbling block is suspiciousness. `I am very social, but I don't have many truly close friends, and even in those friendships, I have trouble with boundaries. I am constantly on the lookout for judgmental intrusiveness. This is a feeling that until this very moment, I have not been able to define. Writing helps me understand my experiences; it is hard to explain just how, but it is both cathartic and instructive.

Strong, close friendships are much easier for me when there is some physical distance between us. When I am in Israel, I can spend hours upon hours with my closest friends. We "fill in the gaps" and enjoy our time together, but both of us know that in a little while I will be flying to the other end of the world, and we'll no longer see each other on a daily basis.

From a physical standpoint, my close friendships are quite interesting. I have a close friend whom I love like a sister, but rarely see. We both know that we will always be close (despite the physical distance), but we also know that we both need space. Space is an important element in my friendships. I can attain great closeness with those who are near and dear to my heart, but at the same time, I require space. I have a hard time with intensive and intrusive people. I admit that this is my own personal flaw. It's not easy to admit that the fault is mine and not theirs.

I have other types of friendships that are equally intriguing. Some of them are many years old; they're not intense, but are marked by mutual love. I know that these friends will always be at my side in times of joy and sorrow. Likewise, I will always be there for them.

Daughters of narcissistic mothers are more sensitive in their relationships. Awareness helps. I have learned to embrace myself, including my more troublesome aspects. My friends accept me as

I am, and I accept them as they are.

If one person sees you, that is enough

There is no easy way to escape the cycle of suppressing and being suppressed. After reading numerous studies, I understand that daughters of narcissistic mothers need at least one person in their childhood to whom they are not invisible. I was fortunate to have a very special uncle; he was slightly odd, and marched to the beat of his own drum. I listened to him; I believed him; I trusted him. He never made fun of me, he expected a lot of me, and he loved me unconditionally. My uncle was there for me, looking out for my well-being, with no ulterior motives.

He was the one who taught me to love reading and writing. He hugged and kissed me, he took me to the seaside to see the beautiful sunsets, he always encouraged me. When I started writing my first book, "Daughter of Iraq," I was living in Israel, but after a few months we came back to the United States. My uncle was a night owl, and during his night (which was my early afternoon), he was at my side as I wrote. Not only did he help me with my research, but he gave me emotional support as I wrote my family's story. He was a writer, too, and could understand the techniques I used and the obstacles I encountered. He also told me that I had unusual talent, and that even though I had four sons, I had to get as much childcare as I could and free myself up so I could make good use of my gift. He was the first one to support and appreciate my writing, and I am eternally grateful for that. Even if I didn't really believe him in the early years, as time passed, I saw that he was right, and that writing was, indeed, my destiny.

It is very hard to break the cycle of narcissism. It would have been much easier for me to fall into the traps that I had grown accustomed to, the traps that landed me in situations that made me feel "at home" – the negative thought patterns that I applied towards myself. It is much simpler to reconstruct what you've been taught, what you've been trained to do for so many years. Nonetheless, I have changed. I am not my mother, even if I see glimpses of her in my behavior.

I created a loving partnership. As a mother, I am nothing like her. I am far from perfect, but I never stop trying, and I learn something new every day. I built a network of loving, inclusive relationships with my dear, affectionate friends and with my female cousins who are special, loving people. They are my soul sisters.

CHAPTER TEN
The Battle for Survival

The need for separation

Daughters of narcissistic mothers face many challenges. One of their biggest difficulties is establishing independence. Narcissistic mothers do their best to keep their daughters tethered to them in any way possible. Make no mistake, though: this is not love. It is a desire for control and self-affirmation. That is why I fought so hard for my independence. I worked with all my strength to build a life for myself, a life built on values that have nothing in common with the values I grew up with. One of the things that helped me was the alienation I felt, and continue to feel, towards my family. One of my uncles used to ask me, "How can you have grown up in your family and come out the way you did?"

My mother's need to control everything made me feel constantly pressured, which in turn led me to rebel and search for my own path. I wanted to discover who I really was. One of my biggest weaknesses is also one of my strengths: when I see something that looks wrong to me, I rebel. Sometimes I have to remind myself that there is no need to rebel; my survival is no longer at risk, and I don't have to fight or hold myself back - it's fine for me to be who I really am. Throughout my childhood, adolescence and young adulthood, this survival tactic helped me separate myself "from her." It allowed me to do things my own way, to choose my own spouse, my own path. Not to simply conform to what she had planned for me.

In a way, I was a good girl. I went with the flow, I was a decent student, and most of all, I never asked for anything more than to be left alone. I placated, helped, supported; I was able to fade into the background. At the same time, there were things that I insisted upon and wouldn't budge on. The first was joining the Nachal unit of the army, and for that I paid a heavy price.

The second thing I wouldn't compromise on, despite what it cost me, was moving in with Amnon (my partner to this day). I didn't give in despite the silent treatment, the vilification, the insults. My decision to join Nachal required unrivaled effort. Living with Amnon also demanded tremendous resolve, but I knew I could count on his strong backbone, something I didn't have in my army days. When I look back on these two issues, my heart is bitter for the young woman I once was. I wish I could hold her to my heart, encourage her, give her strength, calm her down, and assure her that despite my mother, everything would be okay.

The rebellion process wasn't rational. It started with strong feelings of nausea and stomach pain. These symptoms were familiar to me, and I knew that when these feelings set in, I had to fight back. There was no need for an official diagnosis; this was something internal, that guarded and protected me, primarily from myself. I write "from myself" because when a girl is taught that her feelings are wrong, are "in her imagination," the only way to feel the sense of imminent danger is by the feeling she gets in her gut.

Searching for an identity

In the last few nights, I've had two dreams. In the first, I am standing on line at the Ministry of the Interior. Suddenly I see that my mother-in-law is standing on line, too, only she looks about twenty years younger. We talk until my turn arrives. I go up to the clerk, and discover that I've forgotten to bring my passport. He tells me he can't help me and I'll have to come back another time.

I woke up with a bad feeling. So many things came together in this dream. I'm looking for my identity; my passport is missing.

Unfortunately, the scenario of showing up without the proper documents is familiar to me; it is part of my attention deficit disorder. In the dream, I am angry at myself for being so forgetful and scatter-brained, and for having to waste even more precious time. This dream takes place while I am writing this book and pondering my identity.

In the second dream, I am driving down Jabotinsky Street in a Tel Aviv suburb with my mother. For some reason, we momentarily leave the car in the middle of the street. My mother keeps walking, and I go back to the car to wait for her. Suddenly I see her, and I try to lead her back to the car. She is walking on the edge of an abyss; on the other side towers a range of colossal mountains. We can't find the car, and it occurs to me that someone might have stolen it. I periodically pull her towards the sidewalk to keep her from falling, but despite my efforts, she stumbles and falls into the chasm. I try to shout, but nothing comes out. I woke up trembling all over, with a terrible feeling of helplessness. The sensible explanation is that my mother no longer exists, that I have, in a manner of speaking, lost her. I lost her in the process of looking for my own path, and the loss is painful.

A letter to the little girl I once was

A few years ago, in one of my therapy sessions, I was asked to do something that changed my way of thinking forever. I was asked to write a letter to the girl I once was, and to tell her about myself. Only after completing this task did I realize how far I had come. I also realized that it was within my power to go back and comfort the little girl inside me, to soothe that girl's pain. That girl doesn't exist anymore; in her place is a strong, proactive woman, a woman who is no longer the helpless girl she once was. A woman who feels worthy – of love and respect. A woman who knows how to love and be loved. I feel tremendously grateful for what I have every day.

This exercise was an important milestone in my own personal growth. I remember that as a child, I could picture myself as a successful career woman, but I had a hard time imagining myself as married or in a serious relationship. For years, I believed that I would never find true companionship, and I was planning on becoming a single mother. I don't think I realized, back then, that I really was worthy of love and that I could attain both long-term companionship and family. The fact that I have both those things is something I still don't take for granted.

I suggest that every woman write a letter to the girl she used to be. This exercise teaches us women how strong we are, and helps us appreciate how far we have come since our childhood. Writing this letter allowed me to feel love and compassion towards the girl I was. It allowed me to say to her, "Come and see how everything worked out so much better than you ever thought it would. You are a wife and a mother and a writer and a poet and a blogger. You're 'a woman of the world,' as one of my uncles used to say to me. You are independent; you give of yourself and are learning to receive as well, you are aware of your demons but you don't let them define you in any way."

In times of distress, I go back to the frightened little girl and comfort her. I am my own mother, a source of encouragement and strength. This exercise gave me a new perspective, and I suggest that each and every woman give it a try.

CHAPTER ELEVEN
The Different Types of Daughters

Mary Marvel

Karyl McBride discusses the different archetypes of daughters of narcissistic mother. I identified myself very easily. I belong to the first archetype, something I am not at all proud of. (I suppose nobody likes to be categorized.) McBride calls this archetype "Mary Marvel." Like me, Mary Marvel's distinguishing characteristic is achievement, with the goal of proving to herself and the world how wonderful she is. I feel that regardless of how hard I try and how much I accomplish, I never feel good enough, or deserving enough. I never give myself credit for what I do. No matter how much I achieve, it is never enough.

The first time I read about Mary Marvel, I felt like McBride was describing me. I burst into tears and slammed the book shut. Nothing I did mattered – bringing four boys into the world, putting so much into their upbringing, getting five academic degrees, publishing and marketing two books, taking care of anyone who needed care. Always, the question remains: Have I done enough? Am I good enough?

McBride's explanation for this phenomenon is that from a young age, I only felt loved and wanted when I did the right things. The reverse is true as well. My inability to give myself credit is due to the fact that as a child, I always felt I had to prove myself to be worthy of love. When I reached a certain age, I rebelled, but I never stopped striving to be deserving of love.

Girls like me, McBride says, require constant external affirmation; if they get it and it disappears, they have to try something new in order to get it back. Not only is it emotionally draining, it is physically difficult as well. When these girls become women, they often suffer from health problems. In that respect, I've gotten better over the years. I take better care of myself, and sometimes I even take pleasure in my accomplishments. Still, whenever I don't do something I consider important, I deride myself for my inefficiency. Women like us find excuses for every success – "I was lucky," "I was in the right place at the right time." Never "I deserved it." We always feel like it's an act.

The mothers of these girls didn't show their daughters how proud they were of them. They didn't affirm their daughters' character or give them the love they deserved simply by virtue of being their daughters. And even if nobody is doubting them anymore, these girls doubt themselves. They are always comparing themselves to daughters in other families, and sometimes even to their own relatives.

"Why can't you be more like Ofra?" Ofra is my dear cousin. I recently told her about this sentence, which was a constant refrain in my home. I also said that although I could have chosen not to love her as a result, that was never an option for me. I still love her with all my heart – despite everything – because of who she is.

The question I ask myself these days is, When will this end? When will I be absolutely certain that I no longer have to prove myself to the world (and to myself), that I can finally rest? The answer is, I don't know if that will ever happen.

The one who sabotages herself

Another archetype presented by McBride is the daughter who is doomed to failure – the one who sabotages herself. She lacks ambition, frequently numbs her pain through addictions, and stays in destructive relationships. In our family, I suffer from "Mary Marvel Syndrome," whereas my sister falls into this category. When my sister was a girl, her goal was to be a housewife. Then she went to the army, met someone, and married him. My husband and I urged her to continue her studies, and even paid her tuition. She completed her studies with distinction, but afterwards she accepted a job that was beneath her skill level. It would have been different if she had believed in herself. When my sister didn't do my mother's bidding, my mother's explanation was that my sister "had swallowed some amniotic fluid when she was born, and as a result something about her wasn't right." Can you imagine a normal mother saying that about her daughter? My sister wasn't ambitious because she thought she wasn't smart enough, and therefore there was no point in trying.

The two archetypes – the striver and the self-saboteur – are essentially the same woman wearing a different dress. They both feel like they're not good enough. Both pay a steep price, physically and emotionally. They both must learn to depend on their own internal self-approval, rather than always looking for outside affirmation. McBride argues that all daughters of narcissistic mothers sabotage themselves at some point, in some way. During their lifetimes, they will all suffer from one or more of the following problems: depression, anxiety, stress, weight problems, addiction, health concerns, and an inability to forge healthy relationships. They have all internalized the message that they are valued for what they do rather than for who they are; they all have to fight the frustrating voices inside them.

CHAPTER TWELVE
When You Become a Mother Yourself

Building a different model of motherhood

Once I had gotten some distance from my mother and from her influence, I was able to develop a different style of parenting. My intuition (in the first years) and my new awareness (in the later years) enabled me to build a different model of motherhood. Like everything else in life, I learned slowly, and I am still learning. I made mistakes, and I continue to make mistakes every day. In the early years, it was the physical aspect of motherhood that was hardest for me. I couldn't figure out how to cope with it – the sleep deprivation, the difficult pregnancies and births, sick babies. Of course, what I received in exchange was tremendous. After a while, we developed a routine. Those were wonderful, magical years.

As the children grew, so did the problems. Coping with was not easy. It's not easy for any parent, but it is particularly hard for a mother who never learned how to respond to people without hurting them, how to listen to them, how to give them the support they needed, how to notice when something was off-kilter.

I have no easy answers to these questions. In the therapeutic process that I am currently undergoing, I discovered some principles that have made (and continue to make) my life a little easier:

Listen first, then respond.

Ask for advice when you need to, and ask the right person.

If you have a partner, let him help you.

Understand that sometimes we can't help our growing children, although we should always try.

We should always do our best, even if our best isn't all that good. We can make mistakes.

We are all human beings, and we all have feelings. Children who understand that their parents are people, too, can develop empathy towards them and work alongside them to resolve difficulties.

It has been, and still is, very important to me to make it clear to my children that I am not their friend, I am their mother, with all its ramifications. I can have a friendly relationship with them, but they only have one mother, and that is me. I will always love them, with no qualifications, and I will love them for who they are. Once, during a difficult conversation, my son said to me, "You're always going out of your way to tell me you're not my friend. I don't like it." I stood there, shocked; I had tried so hard to give my children the respect and space they deserve. I see friendship as something mutual, in which both people help each other. Friends share hardships, but as a mother, my job is simply to give without expecting anything in return. I am the one charged with listening, with paying attention. Clearly, my son didn't know what I meant. I'm not his friend; I'm so much more. I'm his mother, who loves him without any qualifications. Yes, in normal families there is no need to explicitly say those words – "I'm not my children's friend" – because the distinction is clear, and there is no danger of the mother-child relationship sliding into something more friendly than parental.

Try to respect every child's personal space.

Forgive! Forgive yourself and forgive those around you.

It is easy to write all of these principles, but very hard to practice them.

Every day I remind myself that I am choosing to be the mother I am: I choose love, empathy, mercy, sensitivity. I remind myself that I was not born into these qualities, nor did I grow up with them; I chose them, and continue to choose them, myself.

I remind myself that I am my own person. I am not my mother and I never will be. One of the gravest fears of daughters of narcissistic mothers is that they will turn into their mothers.

I remind myself that I am allowed to make mistakes, and that being weak isn't the end of the world.

I remind myself that I am no longer a lonely little girl. I am allowed to lean on other people, and I have someone I can lean on.

And most importantly, I remind myself that like every other mother, I am not perfect. We are all human.

Building a marriage and a family

The first time I ever experienced true, reciprocal love was in my early twenties, when I fell in love with the man who would become my husband, and he fell in love with me. As far as I was concerned, this was a miracle. I couldn't believe how "lucky" I was, and often, especially during the first few months, I was afraid he would discover the truth – that I didn't really deserve to be loved – and stop loving me.

A short time after we met, we decided to move in together. He was in the army and I was in my last year of university. After a year of living together, we went to England, to work, travel, and save some money on tuition. I found life in England enchanting. Suddenly I was completely independent. I worked, I learned English, I took care of our apartment, and not a word of criticism was spoken. I loved our life there, which reminded me of life on a desert island, and when the year was up, I suggested we stay for another year. He knew, however, that it was important to me that we get married, and he wanted to start school in Israel, so we returned home and settled in Haifa. A year later, we got married, and a year after that, our oldest son, Yotam, was born.

My husband hadn't wanted a child. He wasn't sure he could

make the transition into parenthood, and he was afraid of all the obligations parenthood entailed. He had many sleepless nights during my pregnancy, and was very worried about our financial state. I, as always, "knew" that everything would be fine. After all, I relied only on myself.

I will never forget the day my first son was born. Meeting him for the first time was glorious. He was born in an emergency C-section, so I didn't see him when he first entered the world. When I woke up, he wasn't at my side: he weighed only four pounds at birth and had been rushed off to the NICU. Because he was having a hard time maintaining his body temperature, he would have to stay in the hospital for a few weeks. I couldn't visit him for the first few hours – I wasn't allowed to get out of bed – and only in the evening did they bring me in, on a wheelchair, to meet my son for the first time.

While I was waiting to get out of bed, friends and relatives came to say hello. I remember feeling frustrated because they had seen my child before I had. But now the time had finally arrived. The first time I saw him, he was a tiny bundle, lying on his belly, and he raised his head when I got there. Later on, he would have trouble holding his head up and we would have to do special exercises with him, but that day, when he was less than one day old, he lifted his head to see me. My heart was flooded with warmth and emotion. I looked at my son and whispered, "I can't believe I gave birth to such a beautiful child." Even writing that is terrible; why wouldn't I give birth to a beautiful child?

The weeks that followed were difficult. The truth is, the months that followed were difficult. Yotam was born with undiagnosed asthma, and I was always taking him from doctor to doctor. Still, he was a happy and light-hearted boy. We – his father and I – gave him everything we could. We loved him with all our hearts. Then our second son was born, and we became the parents of two children. Three years later, our third son was born, and four years later, our fourth. We were blessed.

Being a good-enough mother – a mother without a role model

Children do not come with instruction manuals. I remember that, as a young mother, the strongest emotion I felt towards my oldest son was a desire to protect him. I remember the pride and joy that filled my heart when he was born, and the emotional crash that followed. He was very small at birth, and had to stay in the hospital for a few weeks after his birth. After we brought him home, we went through a difficult adjustment period. He had breathing issues, and, as new parents, we didn't know how to deal with it. For the first two years of his life, he slept in our bed; that allowed us to protect and take care of him. My primary instinct was to protect; beyond that, I don't think I was equipped to cope with the transition to motherhood.

In a sense, I think, the early years were physically harder but emotionally easier than the years that followed. I'm not talking about illnesses and health concerns, although there were plenty of those, too. It wasn't hard for me to inundate my children with love and warmth; motherhood enveloped me. I gave up almost everything else; nothing mattered besides my children. I worked part-time, and when my third son was born, I left my job and stayed home. It was important to my husband that I had a life that didn't revolve around diapers, so we hired a babysitter to come a few times a week, and I returned to my studies.

Things I learned from my mother

By now I know that human beings are complex, that things are never black and white. Even with all the trials I went through with my mother, there were positive sides, too. One of her traits that I loved was her desire to be happy and to make others happy. My mother could get up in the morning and announce that we were going on an adventure. As a young girl, I loved this. She was a restless, active mother, and as a little girl I loved our excursions, which often included a trip to the beach.

As a mother of young children, I tried to inject our lives with joy, too. I liked being a mother, and was proud of the important task with which I had been entrusted. I remember some funny anecdotes. Every day, for instance, my oldest son asked if it was his birthday. One day I said to him, "You know, every day is somebody's birthday, so let's celebrate!"

I invited the neighborhood children, baked a chocolate cake and sprinkled colored candy on top, made a pitcher of juice, and we celebrated his birthday, complete with songs and dances. To this day, I consider that one of my most brilliant ideas. My motto was "You only live once." My kids had asthma and allergies. They were sick all the time, and I saw lots of doctors. Maybe too many – all the doctors knew me. I was an anxious mother. I tried to give them my all, while at the same time putting aside time for myself so I had the energy I needed in order to give. I think this was one of the smarter things I did for my children.

All the years I was raising my children, I continued to work, study, or write. I felt that for me, fulfillment meant combining motherhood with other interests that broadened my world.

To avoid replicating my mother's parenting, I went through a long process. I created my own model of motherhood. A new mother's natural instinct is to model herself after her mother, but daughters of narcissistic mothers are afraid to base their behavior on that of their own mothers.

All mothers, by nature, try to forge their own paths, but this is especially true for daughters of suppressed mothers. These women were raised by mothers who couldn't care for them properly or promote their self-esteem. Daughters of narcissistic mothers either try to replicate the motherhood they witnessed or turn away from it; it depends on their level of awareness and their desire to change. Striving to be a better mother to my children helped me create a new kind of motherhood. **In my opinion, if I have learned to be truly attentive to my children, I have triumphed over my biggest demons.**

For daughters of narcissistic mothers, there is no parental support, and thus no emotional support. You were on your own as a child, and so, too, you are on you own as a mother. You have to invent your own version of motherhood. Despite the emotional neglect you experienced from your unemphatic mother, you have to raise your own children with empathy, love, and sensitivity. I recall many moments of frustration and loneliness, even though my partner was always at my side, during both good times and bad. Creating motherhood anew is a complicated mission, especially when you don't have the tools you need. You have nobody to emulate or learn from.

Children, as I wrote, don't come with instructions. The first years are filled with struggles, primarily physical ones. Of course, there are emotional issues, too: the frustrations faced by small children, and, sometimes, by us parents. However, in my opinion, parenthood is even harder when the kids are older. We have much less control over their actions, and their problems tend to be more complicated and more perplexing.

I've been thinking about this a lot recently. About the fact that there were challenging moments when I felt like I was stuck in a maze with no way out. Nothing in my past had prepared me for those moments. I had to face my internal demons while simultaneously taking care of the external problem.

My first reaction to these moments was a sense of suffocation, a desire to die, a feeling that the world had come to an end. Then, after some deep breathing, I was able to think more clearly and to find solutions. When I thought about it more deeply, I realized that the feeling of wanting to die stemmed from two other emotions, shame and guilt, two automatic responses that I had become accustomed to. The reason I say this is that one of the ways my mother controlled me was by humiliating and blaming me, and I absorbed these reactions and adopted them for myself. In situations like these, I tell myself and others: Breathe.... It's not you, it's your mother.

I think I am a good-enough mother, one who isn't perfect but tries to fix her mistakes. While I am an aware and supportive mother, I can also be anxious and fearful. I believe that I transmitted these traits to my children; I wish I could have avoided doing so. Every day I try to be more attentive and more understanding, to know how to set boundaries, to love them, and to make sure they know how wonderful and beloved they are.

PART THREE
AWARENESS, GROWTH, AND COPING MECHANISMS

CHAPTER THIRTEEN
The Behavior of an Abused Girl

I wasn't an abused child, at least not physically. My mother only hit me a handful of times. It's true that one of those times I was seventeen, but my mother had what my relatives called "a volatile hand." The real problem was that she was so unpredictable. That was the reason I was always on the alert, waiting for the "thrashing" that would inevitably happen. It wasn't a physical thrashing, but an emotional one, manifested in insults, denigrations, attacks, disproportionate anger, and verbal abuse. Even now, writing these words makes it hard for me to breathe.

It's hard for a few reasons. First, there's the instant suspicion – "It's just your imagination." I called my husband just to confirm that I am not, in fact, imagining things. These things did happen; he saw these behaviors with his own eyes. Another reason is that "you don't speak ill of your mother." I've gotten so used to being silent, to silencing myself. You're not supposed to say or write bad things about your mother. Instead, you bury your feelings deep inside so they don't explode: end of story. That is my first instinct. Writing this book requires me to get past that, and it's no easy feat. It brings on a whole range of emotions.

My mother's behavior was erratic. Sometimes she would get so angry that she would throw things at us, which usually ended with my mother laughing uncontrollably. I don't remember what my sister said or did, but it prompted my mother, who was standing in the living room, to throw her shoe into the kitchen. My sister crouched down, and the shoe hit a painting and broke the glass. My mother asked her, furiously, "Why did you bend down?" Then she burst out laughing.

When I was a little girl, I didn't know what to expect or when to expect it. After lunch, she always locked the kitchen door. The problem was that right after lunch, we'd be hungry again. What could we do? We snuck into the kitchen and ate! My mother would come out and start hitting us. Usually we'd hide behind the refrigerator, squeezed together like sardines; whoever was closest to her bore the brunt of her anger. Usually the victim was my younger brother, not me. I confess that sometimes when our mother yelled at us and hit us, I blamed it on my brother, even though it was my fault. My mother always believed me, not him.

I was "the good one" and he was "the liar." I was nine or ten, and my brother was seven or eight. My sister was even younger, and wasn't yet part of our circle.

A child who has been battered, or who has experienced any kind of abuse, does not know when the abuse will take place and what will provoke it. Nonetheless, he or she knows with absolute certainty that eventually, it will happen. Unpredictable behavior is a source of constant stress for children, which is why I was, in my mother's words, "a nervous child." I had a hard time at home, I had a hard time at school, and I had a hard time with myself. I wanted to be better, smarter, more successful, and I never felt like I achieved any of these things. My mother didn't compliment or support me, help or encourage me. As for my father… he simply didn't exist.

Cognitive therapist Ilana Sobel[5] lists the personality traits that are associated with child abuse. Among other things, she mentions erratic behavior. According to Sobel, children who grow up with abusive parents grow up with a sense of insecurity, and they are skeptical of all adults. I agree with her.

Beyond the mixed messages that I received, I was a girl who was always watchful, who refused to be controlled or forced to do

---

[5] http://www/macom.org.il/author/ilana/

things against her will, who didn't want to be criticized all the time. When I was little, what I wanted more than anything was for "everyone to just leave me alone," and I tried to stay out of trouble. I did my homework, never asked for help, took care of myself, and generally tried to be a "good girl."

"I have a surprise for Mom." This was what my brother and I would say regarding all the good-will gestures my brothers and I did in an attempt to make my mother happy: tidying up the house, doing the dishes. These acts earned us expressions of support and love from our mother. When we got older, making her happy wasn't so simple. After my father declared bankruptcy, my parents' financial situation was grim. At that time, the only thing that would make my mother happy was giving them money. And I did, if I had the means, or sometimes even if I didn't. When my partner saw my distress, he did everything he could to help my parents. The thanks we received were spoken through tight, twisted lips, and were tainted with the accusation that we were exploiting them. Not much in the way of gratitude or support. The experience left us with a bad taste in our mouths.

CHAPTER FOURTEEN
Coping with Failure

Everybody fails. The secret is knowing how to respond and how to recover. Daughters of narcissistic mothers are acquainted with failure from the moment they enter the world. Their biggest failure, in their eyes, is their inability to be loved by their own mothers simply because they are these women's daughters. From a very young age, they try so hard to merit this love, a love that is supposed to be pure and unconditional, and they always fail. They will experience this kind of unsatisfactory love many times during their lifetime, and they will choose to love men who don't love them back, perhaps in a twisted attempt to reconstruct their fundamental failure in mother-daughter love.

When they are young, these girls don't understand that the problem is a result of an emotional flaw in their mothers and has absolutely nothing to do with them. Their mothers never learned how to love them, just as they never learned how to love their partners. Because the daughters don't understand this, they believe that they do not deserve to be loved. After all, if their own mother can't love them, who could? The daughters feel that they are hiding a dark secret: they have never been worthy of love.

In their eyes, all their failures are simply more proof that "they were right," that they are, in fact, frauds. They are never surprised by their failures, which they see as confirmation of what they've believed all along. Conversely, even the smallest success is considered either a miracle or an illusion.

I have experienced all kinds of failures in my life, large and small. Working on myself has helped me realize that maybe there is something successful in me after all. Over the years, every failure served as another small confirmation of my sense of unworthiness, and even now, when I look at myself from the outside, I am surprised at all the tributes of love, generosity, warmth and praise that have come my way. My first reaction to failure is something to the effect of "I had it coming." It's an automatic response, and I have to take the time to process it before I can accept that I do not, in fact, deserve to fail.

If you don't try, you don't fail. It's important to try, and to fail, too. The truth is, we learn the most from our failures. Failures make us stronger. We fall, we get back up, we keep on going. Most of the time, it is not hard for me to recover from failure. It's a matter of self-talk and life experience. I know that "what doesn't kill me makes me stronger."

I do remember times when I felt like a complete and utter failure, with all its implications. Failure is more than the act of failing; it is the terrible shame that comes along with it, and the fear of looking like a failure in front of other people.

For example, there is a specific event that shook up my entire world for a few days. When I look back on it, it is hard for me to recognize this young girl whose world was devastated by an insensitive man. When I was studying for my master's degree in Hebrew literature, I took a course with one of the field's most eminent professors (who has since retired). He and I had several disagreements about a particular research other. (I admit that my views were somewhat subversive. Still, if I challenged him, isn't that the very point of academia, to look at something from various angles? It's not like I had done something so terrible.) I will never forget a conversation we had in the hall, near the steps of the Rosenberg building, a few months into the course. He told me that I was an "academic disaster." I'm not sure that I was such a disaster, and although today I can look back on this episode with a chuckle, at the time his words broke my heart. I felt tremendous guilt and shame; after all, I was an "academic disaster."

For a few nights, I couldn't sleep. The feeling of uneasiness was the worst part; it settled on my chest and wouldn't give me a moment's peace. It didn't matter what other people said, or how much my partner – the only person I confided in – tried to reassure me. Nothing could ease my overwhelming sense of failure, which was mingled with a keen sense of guilt and shame. Perhaps this man's words were proof that I was indeed a failure – not just academically, but in every aspect of my life. In my mind, this episode was connected to my previous failures and to the pain they had wrought, and I felt badly wounded. In the end, I successfully completed my degree, proving to myself that perhaps I wasn't such a failure after all.

Looking back on this episode, my only thought is that this man had a lot of nerve. Even if he disagreed with me, what right did he have to speak to one of his students like that?

CHAPTER FIFTEEN
The Breaking Point – When Did I Realize I Had a Narcissistic Mother?

The last time I visited Israel, I stayed in a hotel. Every morning I awoke to the sight of blue water and golden sand. I tried to walk along the beach every morning, to listen to the waves, to enjoy them anew; only then would I begin my day. I filled my schedule to bursting, trying to squeeze in as many happy events and experiences as I could. I had been admitted to Agudat HaSofrim, the Israeli association of authors, and I was participating in a ceremony; I presented, alongside my extended family, an annual scholarship at Bar Ilan University; I visited my mythology professor, which moved me deeply; I got together with various cousins; and of course I spent time with dear friends.

I also saw my mother and my brother, along with his family. These were the more loaded, and more painful, components of the visit. I felt like I was walking on eggshells, trying not to fall into any pits but falling nonetheless. The pain accompanied me home, and, as always, it took me some time to calm down, to reassure myself that I was safe with my husband and children, far from my beloved homeland but also far from the pain. My mother did not hesitate to use any means available to get what she wanted, and she didn't care if it caused me pain. To this day, I have not gotten used to this, and it seems I never will. I keep my contact with her at a minimum; I call her only once a week, and I don't share anything personal with her.

Narcissistic mothers are driven only by what serves them best.

They are not empathic or thoughtful. If they want something, they will do whatever they have to do to get it. For many years, my husband and I supported my parents, and now, ever since my father passed away, we support my mother. At one point, we would send her airline tickets once or twice a year so she could visit us. The last time she came to visit (which was more than two years ago), she wanted us to subsidize a visit to Los Angeles – as we had always done – so she could see my father's extended family. That time I refused. She had come during the High Holiday season, a few days before Rosh Hashanah and a few days after we had unpacked the contents of our entire house, having just returned to Seattle from Israel (for the third time).

"Mom," I said, "you came to be with us for the holidays. Why would you go to Los Angeles?" She hadn't gotten her way, and she was very angry about it.

After only a day, there was a dreadful scene, which taught me to be even more vigilant. It made me realize that there was a lot for me to look into, to clarify, to rethink. I was in a terrible emotional state. For the first time, I was truly grasping that something extremely unhealthy had happened to me – and was still happening. Something abnormal, that couldn't be explained as "maternal love." After all, mothers were supposed to want the best for their daughters; how come I didn't have that kind of mother? And how come it took me until I was fifty years old to identify this disease and finally say "no more."

My mother's outburst featured hair-pulling, shrieking, and crying like a wounded animal. It was a completely disproportionate response, and, typically, unanticipated. (She was good at that: over the years I'd witnessed many unexpected behaviors.) After that episode, I couldn't turn the wheel backwards, not even to a minimal connection. Now, I don't feel comfortable including her in my life, my feelings, my thoughts; I am afraid she will use them against me and for her own benefit. Over the years, whenever I shared anything personal with her, she would often use it to make a joke at my expense, to hurt me, and to feel powerful – even when I was a small and powerless girl.

Needless to say, she ended up flying to L.A. She called her

relatives there and told them that we were abusing her, and they immediately sent her a plane ticket so she could "recover." Since then, my mother has not come to visit us. We no longer invite her.

She tries to get to me in all kinds of ways. At first, she tried to turn the extended family against me, but to my relief, she didn't succeed. She is constantly turning my siblings against me, and, as a result, my relationship with my brother is impaired, and my relationship with my sister is non-existent. When my children call her, she tries to turn them against me, too.

In the process of writing this book, my mother and I have fallen into a pattern in which I call her every few days, and she doesn't call me or try to track me down. I ask her how she is and she goes into great detail about what she's been doing and the state of her health. Towards the end of the call, she asks after me; I mutter a few sentences, and the conversation is over. My husband believes that my mother lost all interest in me when I stopped capitulating her narcissistic needs. It still saddens me. I grieve for what I never really had, then go back to my regular life.

CHAPTER SIXTEEN
Coping with Hardship – Struggle as a Learning Opportunity

One of the more painful and complex challenges for daughters of narcissistic mothers is coping with hardship. I feel like I am responsible for everything, things that are in my control and things that are not. I have a similar reaction when I encounter something troubling, or when I run into some kind of wall. I don't give up easily. I have a number of coping mechanisms; I try to look at the problem creatively, to examine it from different perspectives. I end up feeling completely depleted.

In the last few years, I have broken off relationships that were toxic or one-sided, from would not yield anything good. I feel that I tried as hard as I could, but no matter what I did, nothing changed. I ask myself if there was anything I could do to change these relationships, and if the answer is no, I throw up my hands and abandon the relationship. It's not easy, but it's possible. I have found that this is healthier than remaining in a painful and frustrating relationship.

There are certain relationships I would never abandon. If there is an issue with a family member, I don't abandon them because I love them, and I recognize that love comes with its own obstacles and difficulties. I ask myself if there is anything I still haven't tried. It is in these kinds of situations, the ones that pain me the most, that I fall.

I have no idea how other people cope, set boundaries, take care of themselves. I have never been able to do these things, and so I fall. The abyss, while familiar, isn't a pleasant place to be… as I point that out, I don't know whether to laugh or cry. When I get out of the abyss, I can look down and say to myself, "You did it again, you found your way out, and it wasn't as terrible as you thought it would be."

It is in this abyss that I encounter Tali, the helpless little girl I used to be. However, once I remember that I am no longer weak and helpless, I can get out of that frightening place.

It is hard to describe this feeling, but I will try: When I'm "there," I feel like a complete failure. As a mother, as a woman, and definitely as a wife. I feel like I am not good enough, and if that's the case, what's the point? When I say "not good enough," what I am thinking is, "I want to get out of here, to escape to the other end of the world and to stay there forever." Depression is a comorbid condition that I know very well. Depression and desperation. It is strange, because the people around me, those who see me every day, would never guess that I fall into these depths.

Now that I'm taking care of myself, and gaining a better understanding of these processes, it is easier for me to get out of these chasms of anguish. Sometimes it is only a matter of minutes, sometimes it takes longer. Even now that I understand exactly what is happening, and why, I still fall into depression periodically. Although I understand everything, and know that there is nothing further for me to discover, there is still a gap between what I know and what I feel.

The fact that I understand what is going on doesn't necessarily help. At times like this, I find myself thinking, "Why bother? After all, there's no hope that I will never really liberate myself from these shackles, from the feelings of shame, from the belief that I will never be worthy." These are painful thoughts. In order for me to get out of this place, I need a hug or a kind word, and I need to acknowledge that I'm having a hard time and that I need help. It is hard for me to ask for these things, even now. I am used to being strong, to giving to others; it is hard for me to be on the receiving end.

Daughters of narcissistic mothers are used to being the initiators, the doers, the ones who try to "attain the unattainable love." In the last few years, I have decided that I will not do this anymore. I am done hurting myself. I see this as a healthy insight. A "bad morning" is also an insightful morning. It is when we fall into the deepest holes that we learn the most. "What doesn't kill us builds us up." The reason I'm not saying "makes you stronger" is that we are already strong; it is much easier to deal with hardship when you see it as an opportunity to build yourself up.

Two years have passed since I wrote that last paragraph; it's been five years since I understood that I am the daughter of a narcissistic mother. As a result of the work I've done on myself, and the insights I've had, I no longer fall into the darkest pits. Sometimes I am sad about not having grown up with an empathic mother, and I think about how that absence left some scars, but I also realize that it strengthened me, it built me up and shaped me into the woman, and the mother, that I am today. I am not perfect (who is?), but I feel good in my skin.

My senses have grown sharper. I can spot narcissists a mile away, and I keep my distance from them. My friendships have changed a lot over the years, which pleases me, because they are much healthier today. Once we – the daughters of narcissistic mothers – come to certain realizations, once we go through the processes described by McBride, we can lead happy lives, free of depression and negative thoughts about ourselves. We can start to love ourselves, to accept ourselves, and to lead a life free of guilt, pain, and the feeling of never being good enough.

PART FOUR
THE ROAD TO RECOVERY – UNDERSTANDING, ACCEPTANCE, AND RECONCILIATION

CHAPTER SEVENTEEN
The Gap Between Understanding and Feelings

Now that I have grieved, now that I have internalized the true nature of my relationship with my mother, one problem remains: the gap between feeling and thought. I understand that my mother's condition is incurable, that she never loved me the way a healthy mother loves her children, and that she never will. I understand that she has always done her best, and I don't blame her for anything. Nonetheless, the pain remains. Perhaps this exemplifies the gap between the adult woman that I am and the child inside me, who cannot explain the fact that her mother doesn't love her and never did, that she only looks out for her own best interests. That if her mother's desires mesh with those of other people, great, but if it not, she will do whatever she has to do to get her way.

These gaps are hard to bridge, and there is more than one way to bridge them. The processes that I have gone through have given me some useful coping mechanisms. One is a variation on the Serenity Prayer often recited by people struggling with addiction: "Lord, give me the courage to change what can be changed, to lovingly accept what I cannot change, and the ability to tell the difference." I have tried to commit those words to memory: they are wise and, by entrusting me with control, empowering.

Another helpful approach that I have learned is to allow the feelings to surface, face them without fear, and let them go. This technique is known as "mindfulness,"[6] a therapeutic process that combines awareness of one's feelings with meditation, yoga, and being in the moment.

Time heals, too, as does awareness. Understanding what is happening to me helps me cope with the hard times. Whereas my falls into the abyss used to be protracted and terrifying, now they are shorter and more confined. I can bridge the gaps more quickly, and the falls are less drastic. The process is long and hard and, especially, painful, but from an emotional perspective, it is essential.

My greatest challenge as the daughter of a narcissistic mother is my relationship with my children. I recognize that I am not my mother, that I haven't raised my kids the way my mother raised me, but nonetheless, the fear – of hurting the people I cherish most – is unbearable. I know that the fact that I am thinking about this is healthy (after all, such a thought would never have occurred to my mother), so why I am so afraid?

Bridging the gap between logic and emotion, I have learned, is one stage of the healing process. There is hope for daughters of narcissistic mothers. The gap won't always be there, and when it is, it won't be so powerful. Our emotions will not only be felt in our gut, they will also be expressed, because when we are in a place of love and patience, we can express our feelings without fear. A safe place that allows expression will also allow daughters like me to flourish. In this case, flourishing means overcoming unhealthy impulses, building healthier relationships, increasing our self-confidence, and allowing ourselves to have faith in other people. From where I stand, my inability – as a wife, mother, friend – to implicitly trust other people is one of the most painful aspects of being the daughter of a narcissistic mother. The inability to truly trust others makes life difficult for our life partners. It undermines the very idea of partnership, and hurts both sides. This dynamic is unfair to our partners.

Being aware of narcissism helps us make better choices about

---

[6] This kind of attention, also known as mindful awareness or mindfulness, is the psychological process of approaching experiences with guided attention and non-judgementalness, and can be developed through meditation.

whom we should allow into our lives. Sometimes it is easy for me to identify a narcissistic personality, and when I do, I immediately retreat. At other times, I instinctively recoil from someone, and it is only later that I discover that that person is a narcissist. The feeling in my gut clues me in before my heart and mind understand what's going on; after all, this was the first thing I learned, the fundamental lesson that I have counted on all my life. It's never let me down. Not even when I didn't understand it, not even when I wasn't aware of it.

We have to learn to rely on our gut feelings. They don't lie. Nothing tells us more about what is going on emotionally. Gut feelings, and the breathing that accompanies them, indicate danger and hardship or goodness and joy. Gut feelings are our pioneers – they help us consider and strategize our next steps.

After Yom Kippur several years ago, I was engrossed in a book; my mother was sitting opposite me, engrossed in her own book. Suddenly she looked up and said, "I don't think I ever hurt anyone in the whole world." A sentence such as this might best reflect what I experienced as her injured daughter.

CHAPTER EIGHTEEN
The Processes of Emotional Healing

According to McBride, the first step on the road to healing is identifying the problem. After that begins the process of learning about ourselves. "Don't ask what it looks like, ask what emotions it triggers." McBride presents a three-stage model:

Stage one: Understanding the problem cognitively. For me, this happened when I refused to pay for my mother's trip to Los Angeles, when she came to celebrate the holidays with us in Seattle. Her disproportionate and terrifying reaction made me realize that she was sick.

Stage two: Working through the feelings. Allowing ourselves to feel the pain without being afraid of it, and reconfiguring the messages we received in our childhood. Truly mourning the childhood we had with an unemphatic mother. Not being afraid of the pain, but instead, allowing it to flow through us, to envelop us. Even today, this pain overwhelms me from time to time. I am no longer terrified of it; now I give it time and space. I let the feeling float. I can often feel the presence of the little girl that I used to be, and I try to be a mother to her. The changes in my thought patterns will come only after the insights, and after the pain. An example of a shift in my thinking is the

message, "I am good enough just as I am." Negative messages turn into positive ones, and we program our brain to think positively about who we are as women, mothers, daughters, wives and friends.

Stage three: Finding a new definition. The understanding that we are separate from our mothers, the determination to change, the changes that take place inside us. The insights from the previous stage help us redefine who we are. I decided to accept my mother as she was and love her. I also decided to keep my distance from her, and not to welcome her into my day to day life. The hardest decision regarding my mother was not to let her hurt me. I admit that sometimes it's hard for me to stick to this resolution. The desire to receive love from my mother is embedded deep inside me. I understand that she is doing her best, and I try not to expect too much when it comes to our relationship. The decisions I make about myself and my life are linked to self-acceptance and self-love. "I am good enough." I am worthy of love.

All three of these stages are essential, McBride says, but the second stage is the hardest. The worst thing to do, though, is to skip it or run away from it. It is important to allow the feelings and the memories to arise, to encompass us; it is important to sit with these feelings, to allow them to finally evaporate from our system. Only then can we truly be free.

It is at this stage that we accept our mothers' limitations, that we create separation, strengthen the authenticity of our sense of self, build a different, healthier connection with our mothers, and deal with the narcissistic parts of our own personalities so that we don't transmit them to the next generation.

It is important to understand that our mothers damaged us, albeit unintentionally. It is important to understand the nature of this damage, and to make peace with it. It is important to understand that our mothers' inability to love us is their flaw, not ours. Everyone deserves a mother's love, but not only are our mothers incapable of loving us, they also convinced us that we aren't deserving of love.

In my case, this manifests itself in marital love. I was sure I would end up alone; I never thought I'd find someone who would truly love me. To this day, I ask myself how it could be that someone has truly loved me for nearly thirty years. Old habits die hard.

Time and time again, I have to remind myself that the fact that I got used to thinking in a certain way doesn't mean I can't change. It is up to me to continuously "redefine" myself, and to accept that I am deserving of romantic love, parental love from my children, social love from my friends. I am deserving, as we all are.

Allow the feelings of loss to rise up, to envelop you. Don't suppress those feelings, says McBride; we must give them space, because in that pain lies the key to recovery.

McBride lists five stages of grief over the childhood we didn't have, and over the mothers who couldn't love us or validate our feelings:

Acceptance: this is the first step on the road to recovery. We must accept the fact that our mothers had a limited ability to give and to love.

Denial: As children, we had to block out the fact that our mothers were not able to love us, to validate our feelings, or to show us empathy; it was the only way to survive. This denial is what allowed us to grow up and develop.

Bargaining: All our lives, we hoped that our mothers would love us, that something would change. We lived with internal and external conflict. We tried, for years, to deserve our mothers' love, to get our mothers to accept us as we were, without conditions, under any circumstances, as opposed to accepting us because of the things we did.

Anger and rage: We are angry that as children and young adults, our needs weren't met. We are angry at the emotional neglect that hurt us so badly, and at the fact that this neglect caused us, and causes us, to feel like we're trapped in an inescapable cycle.

Depression: We are sad because we have to give up on the idea of the loving, supportive and empowering mother. We feel orphaned, motherless. We mourn the fact that we will never get the mothers we hoped for.

From this point forward, our treatment is largely up to us. Some people will lock themselves in their house, close the blinds, pull the curtains, and mourn quietly, others will write in a journal, and so on. The mourning over the mother who didn't exist, and never will, must be expressed somehow.

Feelings rise up and wash over you, including the sense of guilt that arises when "you think bad thoughts about Mom." It's only natural, McBride says. She suggests that we allow these feelings to come up, and give them space. This holds true for other feelings as well, such as the loss of childhood or the thought that we never really had a childhood, that we were never able to allow ourselves to be girls, plain and simple. I was "very mature for my age," and I couldn't rely on anyone else. Nobody solved my problems for me; I knew that the only one I could count on was myself. It's sad, it's true, but it also made me who I am today. And, of course, it made me stronger. Most problems have their benefits.

Daughters of narcissistic mothers, myself included, have a hard time accepting that they were never really loved by their mothers. They struggle to accept the fact that their mothers didn't protect them. My biggest challenge was expressing all these things outwardly without feeling both shame and guilt, especially now that my mother is old and depends on my goodwill. Emotionally, I waver between the desire to save her and the desire to save myself. When I am in her half of the world, I never know when her hurtfulness will show itself, and what will provoke it. I am always prepared for the worst, and I try to be attentive and compassionate. It is a complicated situation, and coping with it is not easy.

Will we ever be able to free ourselves from this internal and external complexity? **I believe that awareness is a giant step on the road to recovery.** Awareness and understanding, along with allowing all the difficult feelings – including sadness, loss, and desperation – to linger for a while. Step by step, we can let go of all those feelings and try to replace them with more positive thoughts – about ourselves and our abilities, about the love we feel and the love we receive, unconditionally, from the people who surround us. This is called "baseless love." We deserve this kind of love, as do the people around us.

The feelings I had to cope with were complicated, as I have

shared here. I think awareness is the first half of the road to recovery; self-help and self-work compose the second half. Awareness alone is not enough. We have to go through the process of healing and recovery.

CHAPTER NINETEEN
Learning to Set Boundaries and to Trust Your Gut

Boundaries! This might be the most difficult issue for women like us. Nobody ever taught us about boundaries and how to set them. Nobody taught us about the boundaries between a mother and her children, between siblings, between the nuclear family and the extended family. As a girl and adolescent, my privacy was never respected. Everything that happened to me (unless it humiliated my mother) immediately became public property. My mother never hesitated to embarrass, hurt, or denigrate me – anything to keep her in the family spotlight.

As a young girl, I didn't understand the importance of interpersonal boundaries. When I was a little older, around ten, I was considered the "justice and freedom fighter" in our family, but when I look back on my rebelliousness, I see that it was mostly a result of the blurry boundaries I had grown up with. I grew up in a family where you could say whatever you wanted whenever you wanted, however you wanted. Intrusiveness and infringement were absolutely permitted. After having seen the movie "My Big Fat Greek Wedding" numerous times, I can say that I have found an analogy to my experience. The family in the film is presented as intrusive, but in contrast to my family, there is respect for all kinds of choices, and the mother in the movie protects and supports her daughter's choices even when they go against the tradition she'd come from.

That's not the case with me. Boundaries were consistently

crossed, and the result, from my perspective, was a silent war against this encroachment, and a search for peace and serenity. Even in the midst of all this chaos, I searched relentlessly for "who I really was."

As an adult, my boundaries are still breached, but to a lesser extent. I have learned to trust my gut. If I feel that something is wrong, then something really is wrong. Thought comes later; the gut knows first.

The boundaries between me and my mother, me and my partner, and me and my children are extremely important. They preserve me and my surroundings. Instilling boundaries allows my children to grow, to be whoever they want to be, provided, of course, that they do no harm to themselves or others. Love doesn't encroach or intrude, it does not banish boundaries; to the contrary, it allows us and those around us to grow in different directions in an atmosphere of empathy and mutual respect.

Boundaries – Revital Shiri Horowitz

I am scribbling boundaries with a faithful hand
A stable hand is scrawling these boundaries.
The first boundary was the airport
And now it has shifted to the parking lot
And soon it will move again
Up to the first floor
It will open the door and meet you.
Don't be so quick to greet it with a look of fury
And accusation, but feed it with your delights,
I told you – Mom, you do not know
Where you start and where I
End – you are not me and I am not you.
You didn't understand
You flashed me a look of disappointment and hurled your anger at my father.
It is the boundary between us that I am drawing
The hand that draws the boundary is trembling.
I myself don't know where
I start and you end!

The Schiphol airport, June 2006

CHAPTER TWENTY
Between the Hammer and the Anvil – An Aging Mother and Her Adult Children

Not long ago, my mother fell in the street and broke her hip. She was in the hospital for three weeks and returned home in a wheelchair; she would eventually progress to a walker, then a cane.

In the early years, when we were little, every time she needed something, I showed up before she even asked. If she asked and we didn't respond immediately, she would replace the request with a demand, and if her demand wasn't fulfilled, she would switch to shouts, threats, and, frequently, verbal abuse.

In the case of her broken hip, things were different. These days I am considered the "strong" one, while she is "weak." This dynamic saddens me. My mother relies on me, and so, out of moral obligation, I do everything I can to support her. This isn't easy for me.

I don't want to sound ungrateful for all that she gave me over the years. From a physical standpoint, my mother took care of me when I was sick, fed me and clothed me and provided me with a roof over my head. Emotionally, however, not only wasn't she there for me, she was abusive.

When my children were born, my mother came to help. She enjoyed them when they were little, but now that they've grown up, their relationship with her strikes me as a bit peculiar. I feel that she leans on them (at least on those of them who allow her to do so). As a young mother, it was hard for me to hear her scolding my kids; to my regret, I never intervened. I thought my mother was experienced and knew what a mother should and shouldn't do. It was easy for her, I think, to deal with my kids when they were little, and, as a result, they rarely clashed.

For the first week after her injury, I was by her side. She tried very hard to keep any loaded topics out of our conversations; she tried to be pleasant, which made it easier for me to give of myself. It also made it easier emotionally. It wasn't until just before my return flight to Seattle that she brought up the topic of our relationship; she still disavowed any responsibility for our painful relationship. Today, after a few years and a lot of self-work, I can understand her inability to be empathic, to take responsibility, to see things through someone else's eyes. Her reactions didn't surprise me; sadly, I didn't expect anything genuine and good from her. I have no expectations of my mother. I am satisfied with the sense that she can no longer hurt me with her accusations; it's her, not me. This is an important step in my recovery, and I am proud of this achievement.

Being caught between aging mothers and children of different ages is complicated. My mother is aging in such a way that keeping my distance or abandoning her is not an option, but my ways of coping are complex and emotionally exhausting. Alongside this, my children need me just as much. I often have to choose whose needs are more urgent, which is far from simple; sometimes I try to deal with both sides at the same time. When I find myself in this predicament, I try to soothe my spirit in different ways: reading, writing, listening to music, going for long walks, meeting up with friends, anything that will lighten my burden.

A few months later, my mother got sick again. This time I wasn't summoned, as I was already in Israel at the time. My husband and I tried to help, and suggested that she have her gallbladder removed while we were there. She refused, and ended up getting surgery three weeks before the Bar Mitzvah of my youngest son. I asked her to postpone it (it wasn't urgent), and promised that if she did put it off, I would go back to help her recover. There were complications during the surgery, and my mother required a second operation. For two weeks, my suitcase was packed and ready to go while I waited to return home for the Bar Mitzvah. It was a complicated and draining couple of weeks for me. In the end, my mother went back home and slowly recovered; the Bar Mitzvah took place as planned. Not once did my mother ask me about the event. To her, it was of no interest whatsoever. In contrast, every time we spoke, she would repeat the same sentence: "I'm fine, I'll be fine." Needless to say, I had no doubt that she was, and would be, fine. My mother is an expert at taking care of herself.

Another anecdote comes to mind: one of the many times she wasn't feeling well, she asked to be taken to the hospital. My siblings sat with her until one in the morning. When I asked my mother why they stayed so late (after all, they both had jobs and families, and there was no reason for both of them to be there), she responded angrily, "What are you talking about? Of course they stayed with me!" In typical fashion, my narcissistic mother couldn't see anything beyond what was best for her. At times like these, I am grateful for the fact that I don't live near her and I don't have to endure her oppressive hand, her manipulative behavior, her hurtfulness and her excessive need for control.

When a narcissistic mother grows older, she takes everything she can from her children. She takes what they give her willingly, as well as what she demands from them.

A narcissistic mother's behavior is aggressive and inconsiderate. She is unable to acknowledge the needs of her children and grandchildren; as far as she is concerned, she always comes first. She doesn't see the hardships of the people around her, and she can't express empathy for their pain. From her perspective, she is, and always will be, at the center of her children's world, and she has no intention of changing this. She is always very nice to the people outside her family; she understands that by behaving in a pleasant way she can garner more attention and have more of her desires fulfilled. The moment she realizes that her own needs aren't being met, she moves on.

The fact that I don't live near my mother makes it easier to cope with daily life, but it is still hard. My children's needs and challenges, on top of my mother's issues, are complex. Experiences like the ones I mentioned have taught me that it is essential for me to do something small for myself every day: walk in the park, read a book, watch a movie, meditate – anything that brings me pleasure. We have to remember that once a day has passed, it will never come back. Every day, we give of ourselves, but it is just as important for us to replenish our own reservoirs.

CHAPTER TWENTY-ONE
Sibling Relationships in a Family with a Narcissistic Mother

I haven't been close to my siblings since childhood. In my eyes, it was always me versus them. I was the "big sister," the one responsible for their wellbeing. From a very young age, I knew I couldn't allow them into my life. My brother, I knew, would use whatever information he acquired to taunt me and to hurt me. I didn't tell him anything: he knew nothing about my feelings, my loves, my hardships. I had a similar relationship with my sister for many years, and for the last five years we haven't spoken at all, except for issues relating to our elderly mother.

My sister complains that whenever she approached me (which was usually right when I came home from school, hungry and anxious), I would brush her off and ask her to leave me alone. My brother claims I was a "snob." My mother used to badmouth them to me (my sister "was damaged because she had swallowed water during the birth," and my brother was "weak"). She would deride them for not giving her enough help, support and encouragement. When I look back on it now, I see that her behavior was strategically clever. She got exactly what she wanted from me. I was the "savior – the one she could always count on," and at a very early age, I became her "bank." Sadly, aside from using me as their sounding board, my mother and siblings had no use for me. In addition, my mother ruled over us with a mighty hand, and from what I understood, her approach was to "divide and conquer."

When I look back from where I stand now, I realize that the love between me and my siblings was not mutual. I write these words with great pain; who among us doesn't want to love and be loved by the people in our immediate family? Beyond the absence of love, we led very separate lives. I kept my life hidden from them, and their lives were of no interest to me. I left the house at a young age. It was important for me to know that they were alright, but I would never have sat down and had a deep, engaging conversation with them. For as long as I can remember, our worlds were far apart. We understood the world in very different ways.

Although the relationship between my brother and sister is better than either of their relationships with me, there is no real love between them. My sister hasn't invited any family members to her house for many years, and my brother doesn't invite my sister or her family. They see each other at my mother's apartment, and nowhere else. When my mother has a medical issue, the burden falls primarily on my sister. My brother does what he can, but he has small children. I don't live in Israel and my involvement is minimal. My siblings don't keep me informed of what's happening, unless they need something (usually money). There is no give and take, no sharing of feelings – no connection at all.

Sibling relationships are modeled on the relationships we see as children, in our childhood home. Sibling love, self-esteem, respect, altruism – these are all things we learn at home. Sadly, we never learned these things. It is interesting to compare my relationship with my siblings to my mother's relationship with hers. Although they all grew up with a narcissistic mother, they still keep in touch with each other. My mother made choices based on what was best for her brothers. The children and grandchildren were secondary; her brothers came before us.

I find myself mourning the family I don't have. Yesterday, I told my partner that my pain is so overwhelming that sometimes I wonder if I would have been better off staying with my dysfunctional family; at least then I would have a family. Yes, it's a childish thought, but the absence of a family, and of family love, is excruciating for me.

On the kitchen windowsill sits a small picture of the three

siblings. It was taken at the wedding of my mother's youngest brother. I was eight years old at the time, my brother was six, and my sister was three. For some reason, it is still there. I glance at it from time to time, and think about those three sweet, innocent little children who are no more. They have all grown into adults, with all the attendant hardships and pain. The three sweet kids standing so close together in the photo grew into adults who are lightyears away from each other; as of now, it looks like they will never be together again.

A conversation with Karyl McBride – continuing my self-work

One of the services Karyl McBride offers is a day-long one-on-one workshop. I spent a long time deliberating over whether or not I should go. I was curious, but at the same time, I was afraid that meeting her in person would dilute my admiration for her book. Happily, I was not disappointed. McBride is not just an intelligent and interesting woman, she is also a pleasant, empathic woman with a desire to help other women who experienced the same things she did. Over the course of the day we spent together, I felt a certain closeness between us, and a willingness to share my own experiences and emotions with her. She wrote her book out of her personal pain, and as part of her own healing process; I had the good fortune of both reading her book and meeting her in person.

Our meeting generated many insights. I realized that I am still in the middle of the healing process. While I may not have completed the process yet, every day I get closer to total healing. That milestone will only be reached when I am able to be in my mother's presence without losing my own equanimity. It will be reached when I accept, both intellectually and emotionally, that my mother is not healthy; when I no longer fall into her traps; when I can love her in spite of everything.

I am still going through a process with myself, and I hope that the day will come when I will feel and know (again, the heart-mind connection) that I am absolutely fine, that I am doing enough, and that I am good enough, not just to her but to the rest of the world, and especially to myself.

I know that at the end of this process, I will reach an emotional state in which my environment doesn't determine who I am, but I do. I will know that I am in a good place when my feelings are no longer shaped by compliments or criticism. I will be sustained by myself, not by something external.

As the daughter of a narcissist who fits the "Mary Marvel" archetype, my recovery process requires me to work on my internal sense of self. I have to understand that I am good enough, that I "suffice," that my accomplishments deserve recognition, and that the failures that I have experienced, and will experience, are nothing more than opportunities for growth. They do not define me.

When this day comes (and I know it will be soon), I will know that I have closed the cycle, that I have cured myself of this pain and left it behind me. Sometimes I feel like I am just about there, other times I regress into a sense of failure (I have personally failed), a sense of helplessness (I'll never get out of this), and a sense of "not being good enough" (I am infuriatingly mediocre).

All these feelings are familiar to me, and sometimes I find myself sinking back into them, but while it used to take me a long time to get out of those ruts, now I can break the cycle quickly, regain my balance, go back to my emotional core, and remember who I am and the path I have travelled, and am still traveling.

In McBride's workshop, I learned that I am the only person who can cure myself, and that my strength comes from within. She taught me that when times get hard, I must become my own mother. In other words, we – the daughters who didn't grow up with supportive and empowering mothers – can become our own empathic, gentle and loving mothers. We can recreate, in our hearts, all the maternal qualities that were withheld from us, and make ourselves stronger. This isn't to say that we are confronting the world alone; on the contrary, there are loving and supportive people all around us, and we can allow them to help us. The "maternal" support, however, that we always seek and never find – that can only be found inside us.

When the workshop was over, I left McBride's office with a sense of contentment that I hadn't expected. I knew I was good enough, and I knew that I wasn't the only one who felt that "something was not right" in her relationship with her mother." I knew that many women felt, and continue to feel, the same emotions that I feel, and I knew that I have the power not only to take care of myself, but to help other women as well.

Who loves me anyway? Dr. Anat Aderet

Once, a small
Boy, whose mother and father
Were always busy with
All kinds of things,
Suddenly
Felt lonely and sad.
He left his house
And went into the street, and thought
About how much
He wanted someone
To love him,
And it didn't matter
Who.

The boy met
A small cat,
And asked him:
Little cat, do you
Love me? Meow, replied
The cat, yes, I love you,
And he stroked him with his tale,

And if you give me milk,
I will love you
Even more.

The boy saw
A bird flying
In the sky
And asked her,
Chirp, chirp, do you
Love me? Yes,
She chirped back
And if you build me
A nest, I will
Love you even more.

The boy met
A beautiful
Flower blooming
In the very middle
Of the park. The boy
Asked it, too: Flower,
Do you love me?
Then the flower answered,
Yes, I think so,
And if you move
And don't block
The sun, I will
Love you even more,
Little boy.

And then,
The moon came out,
The boy went back home
And his mother and his father
Kissed him
And the boy asked them,
Do you love me?
And they said,
Of course we do,
Very much. And the boy asked:
Why? And they said:
Because you are
Our son, and they
Gave him a hug.

So love your
Dear ones, just like this,
Hug and kiss them,
For no particular
Reason, simply
Out of love.

THANK YOU

Thank you for taking the time to read *It's Just Your Imagination*. If you enjoyed it, please consider telling your friends and posting a short review. Word of mouth is an author's best friend and much appreciated. Again, thank you.

~ Revital Shiri-Horowitz

OTHER WORKS BY REVITAL SHIRI-HOROWITZ

Daughters of Iraq - Daughters of Iraq is the compelling story of three women from the same family. It is the story of emigration from Iraq to Israel as experienced by two sisters: Violet, whom we learn about through a diary she kept after being diagnosed with a critical illness, and Farida, whose personality unfolds through her relationship with her surroundings, and with herself. The third character is Noa, Violet's daughter and a student, a young woman in her twenties who is searching for meaning. Noa embarks on a spiritual quest to the past, so that she can learn how to build her life in the present and the future.

Hope to See You Soon - Tel Aviv and Seattle. A woman who does the unthinkable. Two best friends living far apart, and how that separation shapes their lives. Is the grass really greener on the other side of the fence? Which comes first, family or country? And how far should we go to secure our happiness? In "Hope to See you Soon," author Revital Horowitz challenges her readers to confront these questions, and to grapple with the meaning of friendship, family, and country- the meaning of life itself.

The novel, which will resonate with all its readers but particularly with anyone who has ever lived abroad, is full of moral challenges and cross-examinations. The past mingles with the present as the friends exchange letters over the years. The characters are compelling and sympathetic. You won't want to put this book down until you've reached the end.

BONUS EXCERPT
The Daughters of Iraq

Chapter One: Noa Rosen

Noa rushed out of the apartment, which she shared with a roommate. She hadn't heard the alarm go off, even though it had buzzed for quite some time. She'd woken up in a fog only to discover that it was 8:20. In less than an hour, she'd be starting her "Introduction to Jewish Philosophy" exam; it was an important test, and she had been studying for days. All night she had tossed and turned, and when she finally did fall asleep, she'd had a bizarre dream. The course material mingled with her daily life: angels were climbing up and down, gathering around her in a circle. Michael and Gabriel, she thought. Her brother Guy was in the dream, but as a small boy with angel wings on his back. Her mother was in it, too. She wrapped Noa in her arms, and Noa felt wonderfully safe. She told her mother that she missed her very much, and that she was glad her mother had finally come home. Noa noticed that her mother's hair had grown back; the last time they had seen each other, she'd been wearing a wig. When she tried to touch her mother's hair, it turned into the Kabbalistic chart that she had memorized the previous night. The sound of the alarm interrupted her sleep, and she woke up trembling all over.

Sitting on the bus, bleary-eyed, she tried to interpret the dream. Angels going up and down, and Ima, and Guy… no wonder she'd woken up more tired than she'd been the night before. A multitude of thoughts darted through her mind, and she tried to make some sense of them.

Noa was in her second year of studying Hebrew literature, and she supported herself by working in the university library. She believed in financial independence, and she refused to be a full-time student unless she could pay her own tuition and living costs.

After the death of her mother Violet, Noa had extended her tour of army duty. She wanted to stay in the same environment, and she was glad to be far from home. When she completed her army service as a lieutenant, she decided to save up for college, and to see a little bit of the world. She worked as a waitress for awhile, then traveled with Barak, her boyfriend at the time. When she decided it was time to start studying, she took on a heavy course load and worked in the library as many hours as she could.

Ever since her mother had passed away six years earlier, Noa had not been at peace, and pangs of guilt haunted her without mercy. Her mother's death had come as a shock, and she was still struggling to come to terms with it.

Noa never believed that her strong, vigorous mother would succumb to the cancer that had struck her when Noa was fourteen. Violet's stubbornness had bought her a few more years in the heart of her family, but Noa, like every other teenager, was busy with her own affairs. She didn't understand that her mother was living on borrowed time, and so she hadn't taken her place at her mother's bedside.

Violet, for her part, had no desire to draw her daughter into her pain, or into her struggle to deal with her illness. She herself didn't believe that the illness would prevail in the end. Even when the doctors talked about her critical condition, she refused to accept their evil decree and continued to broadcast messages of reassurance to all those around her. Violet had not prepared her daughter for the worst possible outcome.

One fall morning, Violet was undergoing a routine round of chemotherapy, and all of the systems in her body collapsed. Noa was summoned home from the army, and Guy was taken from school to the bedside of his dying mother. That same night, without saying goodbye to her husband and her children, Violet left this world and passed on to the world to come, leaving her loved ones broken and aching. Noa was only twenty when her mother passed away, and because she had not been at her mother's side during her final days, she felt that a part of her soul had died.

Dejected, Noa sat on the bus, which was crammed with university students, teenagers, and old people. She rested her nose and forehead against the frame of the open window. Even though it was only June, the mornings had already become oppressively hot. People pushed up against each other, and the smells of sweat, spices, and fresh vegetables from the market blended into a thick odor. Noa didn't notice the chaos, didn't hear the voices, didn't smell the smells; she didn't pay attention to the trip at all.

In her head, she was floating to other destinations. She had been doing this since her childhood, whenever she found herself in an unpleasant situation. The smell of spices and fresh vegetables made her think of her Aunt Farida, her mother's sister. Farida had always looked out for her; she had given her love freely and without conditions. No matter when or where, Noa could always count on her for a warm word, an embrace, a reassurance. Farida's image rose before Noa's eyes. Her husky voice- a testament to her many years of smoking cigarettes- was soothing, and it brought a faint smile to Noa's lips. In her mind, Noa saw her aunt's stout body, and she heard her heavy Iraqi accent. Farida was Noa's favorite aunt: a gentle and kind soul in a large, ungainly body.

Farida was truly an enormous woman: her breasts sagged heavily upon her gargantuan belly, falling beneath her hips. Noa yearned for her aunt's warm touch, which had quietly protected her over the years. Aunt Farida's demeanor was kind and reassuring: her nose was as wide as her heart, and her forehead was plowed with wrinkles which vanished whenever she smiled. She had a large chin with a dimple in the middle, and dark, sympathetic eyes that always looked tired. Aunt Farida's life had not been easy, but despite all her hardships, she exuded optimism and love. Aunt Farida was large in size, and she was larger than life; thinking of her made Noa smile. Just like one of those Bozo the Clown punching bags, she would fall down and get back up. She was always so encouraging, a safe haven in Noa's turbulent life. Noa had no idea what she would have done without her.

Noa was still trying to decipher her strange dream. She understood that it had something to do with the exam, but she couldn't remember the obscure words that her brother had whispered to her. Noa tried to find a connection between the dream and her current preoccupations and thoughts. Her mind returned to her mother, and her grief was unbearable. Her eyes welled up with tears when she imagined what her life would be like if she could share her thoughts and her struggles with her mother. Noa yearned for the comforts of a real home. Her childhood house was nothing like it had been before her mother had died; in fact, it was barely recognizable. Every inch of the house, it seemed, was drenched with sadness. The joys of living that had once filled the house, that had almost burst through its walls, had disappeared; now the walls reminded her of a castle that had been deserted by its queen and was on the verge of collapse. The study, that had once been crammed with papers, had been abandoned; the fragrance of spices was gone, too. And Aba had immersed himself in his own affairs. Since he was left to himself, he buried himself in his work, and, in the last two years, in his studies. He made a point of cooking dinner every Friday night, trying to maintain the family's long-time tradition of eating together once a week. But without Violet, the meals just weren't the same.

Noa wanted to fall into Farida's arms and rest there, she was so tired. Maybe she'd go visit her after the test, she thought. She had no plans for the rest of the day, and the test would only take three hours. If she caught the 12:00 bus, she would get to the village within two hours. She had the whole day; yes, that's what she would do. She would call Aunt Farida and ask her what was for supper. She'd get on the bus that would wind its way through all the streets, eventually taking her to her aunt's house. The smells of familiar and beloved Iraqi dishes filled her nostrils… Aunt Farida would spoil her and feed her and, most likely, send her home with packages of food to keep her going for the rest of the week. Yes, she'd call her after the test. Noa remembered the times she had shown up at Aunt Farida's house, sad and forlorn like a rebellious teenager. Farida was always there for her, always smiling, always waiting with pots full of good food and luscious pastries- all the comforts of a real home.

When the bus reached its stop, Noa woke up from her daydream. She hadn't noticed the bus moving, or passengers getting on and off. She had no memory of Bus 25 following its usual route from her apartment on the Street of the Prophets to the gates of the university. Noa almost forgot to get off at the stop closest to the Gilman building where the test would be given. At the entrance to the university, she slammed her leg into the security guard's table and stifled a scream. She plodded up the stairs, one step at a time. Only when she sat down for the exam did she feel her distracted mind shift into focus. All the daydreams that had kept her company that morning went into remission, clearing her mind for the concentration that the test required. Noa bent over the paper, ready for her mission. Completely absorbed in the text before her, she took a deep breath and shook out her muscles. It was as though everything else had been leading up to this test. She had spent days and nights studying, going over the material again and again, and now that the "day of judgment" had arrived, she was prepared, like a soldier ready for battle.

Noa lifted her head and looked around. She saw the heads of the other students, bent over their work. She looked up at the preceptor who was walking past her, offering her a candy and wishing her luck, giving her a reassuring look, as if she were reading her mind. She could do this, Noa thought. If she just relaxed a little bit, the lines of text would stop dancing around in front of her. Noa took some deep breaths and looked back down at her test. When she carefully read the first question, and the four that followed, she knew that her hard work had paid off. She understood what she had to do, and she began to write.

Chapter Two: Farida Sasson

That morning, Farida wasn't sure if it made sense for her to do her usual Sunday errands. She had both a daily routine and a weekly routine, and she tried to stick to them; she knew that if she fell behind schedule, the pressure would be too much for her. Sunday was supposed to be haircut day. After spending all day Saturday cooking, by Sunday morning she usually looked haggard, and her fine hair was usually saturated with kitchen smells. That's why Sunday was her day to head downtown for her weekly salon visit. On that particular Sunday morning, however, she was reluctant to leave the house. The heat was oppressive, and the newscasters were once again talking about terrorist attacks. In order to get to her appointment, she would have to wait for Bus # 15 which came only once an hour, take the bus to the center of town, and then walk to Shimon's Salon, which was next door to Chaim the Moroccan's butcher, right below the new Chinese restaurant. Because of all the talk about bombs, Farida was reluctant to take the bus, and so- after much deliberation- she decided to stay home and cook okra patties for her grandchildren who were visiting the following day.

She rinsed the okra and removed the stalks, sliced an onion and sautéed it. While she worked, her thoughts drifted to Baghdad, the city of her birth. Farida remembered the large houses with the enormous courtyards, designed to accommodate prodigious families like hers. Each wing of her house was inhabited by a different family: Aba, Ima, Violet, and Farida herself, the youngest daughter, lived in one wing; her sister Farcha, along with her husband Sammy and their three children, lived in another; her brother Anwar lived in a third wing with his wife Yasmin and their three daughters; in yet another wing lived her sister Chaviva with her husband Yaakov and their five impish kids. Farida loved her nieces and nephews as if they were her own siblings, perhaps because they were closer to her age than her own brothers and sisters. She and Violet were the youngest of the brood. Georgia, their mother, had given birth to Chaviva, Farcha, and Anwar at a very young age. She had then had two more children, both of whom died in infancy. After many years the two girls were born- less than two years apart. These girls brightened her heart and brought her solace. By the time Farida and Violet were born, they were already aunts to Edward, Chaviva and Yaakov's oldest son. The rest of the nieces and nephews came later. Eddy, as he was called by everyone, was born a year before Violet; a year and a half after Violet was born, Farida came into the world.

Farida remembered how she, Eddie and Violet used to sneak out of school. They would look for a horse-drawn carriage, jump on the back, and hitch a ride through the streets of Baghdad. If the driver caught sight of the kids, he would strike them with his horsewhip and curse them for riding on his carriage without paying the fare. Later on, when they were a little older, they would race to the nearby Chidekel River where they'd take off their clothes and swim in its cool waters, free from trouble and pain, splashing each other and laughing endlessly.

During the summer, when Baghdad's rivers dried up, tiny islands would surface- *jazira*, they were called- and the children would go there to search for water creatures which they would pick up and closely examine. Then they'd get dressed, pack up their bags, and return home, pretending they were coming straight from school. Because they went to the Jewish school, the teachers all knew the parents, and if they ever suspected that something wasn't quite right, they would pop in for an unannounced visit. The kids knew that when a teacher came to the house, the punishment would be severe. They paid the price of their adventures willingly, however, taking comfort in the knowledge that they would return, again and again, to these moments of pure delight.

"*Ach,*" Farida sighed, "it's a shame, *walla*, it is such a shame." She was talking to herself in the empty kitchen, where only the pots and pans could hear her thoughts. "It's a shame we couldn't have had that kind of life together." Farida and Eddie had had a special closeness during their childhood, which later blossomed into a full-fledged love. Farida's heart clenched inside her at the thought that she and Eddie couldn't get married, couldn't bring children into the world. "He was so handsome…." She sighed once again. "And his eyes, don't get me started, those eyes…." She continued to ruminate, first out loud and then in silence, remembering different episodes from her life which made her feel his absence, and his loss, more acutely than ever.

She sliced up the okra, and the vegetable's color made her think of his smart green eyes. Tears rolled down her cheeks. She wiped them with the edge of her sleeve to keep them from dripping onto the cutting board, and she put down her knife. For a long time she stood there, stooped over the cutting board, until the wave of emotions had passed; then she stood up, took another stalk from the platter on the counter, removed its rough edges, and returned it to the platter. When she had finished preparing the vegetables, Farida dipped her hands in water and began to prepare the filling for the *kubot*- the semolina pockets. She took some ground chicken mixed with parsley and spices, placed it on the dough, and rolled the mixture into small balls, which she dropped into a steaming pot of water.

In her mind, Farida returned to the Iraq of the mid-1940's. She remembered how Yasmin, Anwar's wife, had finally given Anwar a son after three daughters, how they had celebrated his birth with a *chalri*- a traditional Arabic party with belly-dancing. The *chalri* took place on the seventh day after the child's birth- the day before his *brit*. Farida's parents had invited relatives from all across Baghdad, Hilla and Basra. All the important people in the Jewish community had been invited. Farida's mother Georgia was a pillar of Baghdad's Jewish community; she came from a family of well-known rabbis, and it was considered a great honor to be invited to one of her parties. Nothing was overlooked; the best musicians and singers were summoned to the *chalri*, along with a famous belly dancer who strutted before the wild eyes of the spectators. Some of the men stuck bills into her belt and her bra, and everyone sang, danced, and showered the new baby, his parents, and his whole family with blessings.

After the birth of her son, Yasmin took to her bed and barely got up for forty days. At that stage, her job was to take care of the new baby, and to rest. The women from her extended family waited upon her, fed her, and tended to all of her, and her baby's, needs. They took care of the mother, the house, the other children, if there were any, and the husband, so that the mother could regain her strength and take care of her family. All this the women did with great joy and unlimited generosity.

That was a good year: a charmed birth as well as the Bar Mitzvah of Eddie, the first grandson of the family, and everyone's darling. And despite the fact that he was almost thirteen, and that she was not yet ten, and despite the fact that this was usually when boys and girls from the same family were separated on account of the new, strange, amorphous tension between them, Farida remembered that they couldn't stand being apart, not even for a day. When they did see each other, they secretly pledged their love for one another until the end of time.

On the day of the baby's birth, Eddie, Violet and Farida were given an important task: they were sent off to tell all their acquaintances about the birth of the child. Once word got out, all the women- relatives, servants, Arab and Jewish neighbors alike- began to trill loudly in celebration of the happy event. Those who hadn't yet heard the news now understood: something wonderful had occurred in the Twaina household.

At the conclusion of that festive day, the merry trio split up as usual, and went off to sleep in their separate homes. It was a stifling Baghdadi night. In the height of the summer, when it was too hot to sleep in their beds, people camped out on the roof. Farida and Violet, along with their parents, slept on the roof of one of the wings of the big house, while Eddie and his family slept above another wing. After the excitement of the day, Eddie, Violet, and Farida were having trouble falling asleep; they gazed at the lovely full moon shining in the distant sky, at the innumerable stars. They were filled with a sense of great satisfaction and indescribable joy. A new son had been born into the family, and they were all part of this creation.

Chapter Three: Violet Rosen

Monday, October 15, 1986

"Violet! Violet Twaina!" a voice thundered. "Come here right this instant!"

"My father's calling me," I said to Naima, my best friend. "Don't go anywhere. I'll be right back." I ran up the narrow stairway that led to my family's house, and as soon as I looked into Aba's eyes,

I knew I was in serious trouble. My heart froze.

"Violet Twaina!" My father was fuming. He was standing up, rocking on his heels, and his hands were buried deep inside his pockets. "Violet, Mrs. Chanukah called from school. She said you talked back to Mrs. Zbeida today." His words were accompanied by his terrifying glare, a sure sign that a harsh punishment awaited me.

"What are you talking about? I didn't do anything," I lied, crossing my fingers behind my back, desperately trying to wheedle my way out of this situation.

"Don't tell me stories, Violet," my father said. "I know you're lying, and I know that you talked back! Mrs. Chanukah doesn't call parents out of the blue and waste their precious time. She told me that Mrs. Zbeida asked you to stop talking, and that you told her that you hadn't been talking and that perhaps it was time for her to get her hearing checked once and for all because this wasn't the first time that she blamed you for something you hadn't done."

"That's not true. That's not how it happened! She's always accusing me of things I didn't do. I hate that teacher," I blurted out. "She's always picking on me for no reason. She's very rude to me. She told me to shut up, and I told her that I hadn't said anything. And," I continued, unable to stop myself, "I said it very politely. All I said is that she must have misheard, because it wasn't me. If you want, you can ask Naima," I concluded, dragging poor Naima into my scheme.

"Go find Naima and tell her to come upstairs right away." My father's voice was angry; I could tell he didn't believe me. I went down and called to Naima, trying to think of what I could give her in exchange for her cooperation.

"Naima," I pleaded, "My father wants to ask you something, and you really have to help me. If you do what I tell you, I'll give you Fahima as a present." Fahima was my most beautiful doll. She had long flowing hair which I loved to comb, and several changes of clothes that my mother had sewn especially for her.

"Fahima?" Naima asked in disbelief. "Are you saying that if I do what you say, you'll really give her to me?"

"Yes, I swear, I'll give her to you." I raised my hands to my heart and looked right into her eyes. I knew she wouldn't be able to resist. "That vicious teacher Mrs. Zbeida, she's always getting me into trouble. You have to tell my father that I didn't say a thing in school today. Tell him that everything I told him is true."

"*Wai li,*" exclaimed Naima, grinning broadly. "The way you spoke to her! The whole class was rolling on the floor."

"*Ya'allah*, come on," I begged her, "I promise I'll give you Fahima, alright? What's the big deal?"

"OK, fine, I'll do it," she promised. "But what if your father finds out that we're lying?"

She was right to be worried, but my style was to jump headfirst into the icy water, then think about it. "I don't know," I snapped. "It's better not to dwell on that. Let's go, he's waiting for us."

We went upstairs. Aba was sitting in the big red armchair, which was covered by an embroidered fabric flecked with real gold. When we walked into the living room, he fixed his most menacing gaze on us, then turned towards Naima. Normally my father would have asked after Naima's family, but this time he got straight to the point:

"I understand something happened in school today."

Naima stared at the floor, choking on her words, then mumbled her reply. "Yes, Mr. Twaina. A lot of things happened in school today. Which one do you mean?"

"I understand that Mrs. Zbeida got angry at Violet during class today. Can you tell me exactly what happened?"

Naima, who knew exactly which incident he was talking about, tried to fulfill her part of the deal. In a voice not much louder than a whisper, she responded, "Um… um… Mrs. Zbeida didn't get angry at Violet at all."

I hadn't thought of this. My father was smarter than me; instead of offering my version of the story for her verification, he allowed Naima to make up her own rendition.

"That's not what the principal, Mrs. Chanukah, told me!" he seethed.

"Mr. Twaina," Naima said, valiantly trying to defend me, "Violet is such a good student, so quiet and serious. Nobody could ever complain about her. She sits so nicely in class. She pays attention, she doesn't talk, and she always does her homework. It doesn't seem possible that she did anything wrong. Mrs. Chanukah must have gotten her mixed up with this other girl who's always bothering her, and called you instead of the other parents."

Even I could tell that she was pushing it. And Aba....Aba, who knew me very well, who knew that I could never be the angelic little girl that Naima was describing, couldn't decide whether to laugh or cry. Realizing that Naima would be of no help, he called for his driver and sent Naima home. I knew exactly what would happen next. This is it, I thought. I'm doomed. A week under "house arrest." No going out to see other people, and nobody coming to see me. I wasn't afraid of the beatings. Whenever my father hit me, I imagined that Eddie, Farida and I were jumping into the river, and all I was feeling was the touch of water on my skin.

This time, my father didn't even yell. He glared at me, then spoke:

"I know you, and I know that you talked back to your teacher. Not only did you lie to me, but you made Naima lie to me as well. You are a bad girl, and you have no respect for anyone, and you don't care about anything. The only thing you care about is yourself. So now I'll show you exactly what you are. Go to my belt closet, and bring me my thickest belt. Go on, I'll wait for you right here. If you trick me again and bring me a different belt, I'll beat you with both of them."

I went up to my parents' room crying bitterly, knowing that nothing could help me now. The other children saw me crying, but didn't say a word; they were already used to these scenes. I was the only girl in my family who got beaten endlessly, and everyone knew why. I was the rebellious child. I dodged responsibilities and I broke limits. I wasn't afraid of anything, and I did whatever I wanted. I lied constantly, with no remorse. I ran away to the river with Eddie, I talked back to the teachers, I skipped classes, and I stole money from my mother's drawer for candy. In other words,

I knew how to live, and I didn't let any person, or any consequence, dampen my adventurous spirit.

I was beaten quite severely that day, and if my mother hadn't pleaded with my father to stop, I am sure he wouldn't have stopped on his own. My back hurt, my bottom hurt, and I couldn't move. Needless to say, he went on to tell me that until Eddie's Bar Mitzvah, which was ten days away, I could only leave the house to go to school, and I had to come straight home. I couldn't play outside, and I couldn't see my friends. Aba's driver would pick me up every morning, then bring me back home. None of this managed to break my spirit, because I knew that all I needed was a little patience; then I could go back to doing whatever I wanted. I never gave Fahima to Naima. I told her she hadn't fulfilled her side of the bargain, and that she'd gotten me into even more trouble. Back then, that kind of behavior was typical of me.

Chapter Four: At Aunt Farida's

"Hello my sweet girl, my soul, God should bless you, how did you know I was thinking about you all morning?" Farida hugged Noa and planted wet kisses on both cheeks. "I missed you, what were you thinking, why didn't you call me all week?"

"Hi, Aunt Farida," Noa said, sinking into her aunt's soft, warm body, wrapping her arms around her, drinking in warmth and security. "I was so busy, you know how it is.

Work, school, exams… even today I had an exam. You see? I came to visit you as soon as I could. What's that fantastic smell? Okra?" She headed into the kitchen, following the scent.

"Your sense of smell is very acute, a blessing on your head. I'm so glad you came, there's okra with meat dumplings, just what you like, and as you can see, I'm also making *machbuz*," she said, tempting her niece with the promise of Noa's favorite Iraqi pastries. "Eat, eat," urged Farida, taking a tray out of the oven, "and when you go, I'll send you home with a bag of Purim goodies," she added, laughing. "Now tell me, Noa, how was the test?"

"It was fine." Noa let out a loud sigh, popping a piece of cheese pastry into her mouth. "I'm glad it's over. This exam was weighing on me. There was so much material, you can't even imagine. I spent so much time studying at my desk that my behind was starting to hurt...."

"*Nu*, I'm sure you did well. With your mother's intelligence and your father's good looks, you'll go far," Farida said, clasping her hands together.

Farida's words made Noa laugh. "Wait a minute, are you trying to tell me that my mother was ugly and my father was stupid?"

"God forbid!" Farida said, wringing her hands, spitting, doing whatever she could to disperse any evil spirits that might be loitering outside her door. "Your mother, *allah yirchama,* was beautiful *and* good *and* smart, and your father, was there anything he couldn't do? *Ya'allah,* come here and sit down." Farida pointed to the empty chair across from her. "When you're finished eating, we'll get to work. You see," she said with a smile, "I already made the dough for the *machbuz.*"

"I came at the right time," Noa said, laughing. "As if you really need help.... Actually," she pronounced, "I'm in the mood to bake something together." Noa leaned back into her chair. "Do you remember, when I was little, I would spend my vacations with you, and Sigali and I would help you bake? We each had our own regular job: Sigali was in charge of rolling the date spread into little balls and stuffing them into the dough, and my job was to dip the dough in water and sprinkle it with sesame seeds."

"Yes, of course I remember, that's what's called 'Tena Maca',." Farida's laugh disintegrated into a coughing fit, and she cursed her cigarettes.

"Tena Maca? What's that?"

"Ah," Farida sighed. "Tena Meca is a code word for babysitting. If one woman needed a little peace and quiet, she would ask her neighbor to give her children a Tena Maca- to keep them occupied for a few minutes... Oh, baking was such a Tena Maca." She waved her hand. "You and Sigali helped me in the kitchen, and

Uncle Moshe got to rest a little bit. *Ya'allah*, my sweet girl, even though Uncle Moshe's been gone for awhile, and nobody in this house needs a Tena Maca, I'll still let you help me. But first, have a drink, taste my okra, I even have some rice all ready. Work can wait a little bit."

Farida scanned her niece from head to toe. "What's the matter, Noa'le? You don't look good to me today." She piled her freshly-baked treats onto Noa's plate. "What, you're not sleeping at night? You've lost a little weight. What's going on, aren't you eating?"

"No, Aunt Farida, really, I'm fine. And what's this about losing weight? I wish." Noa gave her aunt a bewildered smile. "Actually, it wouldn't be so bad if I lost a few pounds. It's this test," she added. "I didn't sleep well last night." Noa sat next to the little table. It was loaded with an abundance of delicacies, as if Farida were planning to feed an entire regimen. "Is someone else coming?"

"No," Aunt Farida said, a little sadly. "I wish."

"So who are you cooking for?"

Aunt Farida sat in the chair opposite her, looked around, and sighed. "I don't know how to cook for two people. Only for an army, that's how it is. It's not so awful; whatever's left over, you can take back to your apartment." She gazed out the little kitchen window.

Outside, children were playing. The sounds of their laughter tugged at Farida's heartstrings. She remembered other days. For a moment there was a strained silence between the two women. Each of them seemed to be remembering scenes from the past: a house buoyant with life, crammed with people. So much had changed in recent years, they both thought, each of them yearning for a time that was long gone.

Sigali had gotten married and was the first one to leave the house; then Oren got married. Sigali had two sons before leaving her husband. "It killed me," she had said, "that he wasn't doing anything with his life." Oren was living in Nahariya and rarely visited. Sigali lived near Aunt Farida, and whenever one of her kids got sick, she would bring the child over. Most of the time, though,

Sigali was busy with her own affairs; she was a single mother, it wasn't easy. And Uncle Moshe… Uncle Moshe had died two years ago. Only Farida herself remained, and being alone was not easy for her.

For many years, Uncle Moshe was out of work, and the family lived off social security. Uncle Moshe was, as people used to say, "heart-shocked." He had gone off to war as one man and returned as another, shattered into slivers. He was never able to get over the trauma of war. From fragments of conversation over the years, Noa had collected an assortment of images, and from those images she was able to create a complete picture.

Uncle Moshe had been taken to fight at Sinai. He was the platoon's chef, and one morning he woke up from a dreadful dream, soaked in sweat. In his dream, all the men in his platoon were killed in a surprise attack by the Egyptians. Uncle Moshe had just climbed out of his sleeping bag and was looking for a quiet spot where he could pee and calm his nerves when the bombing started. His friends didn't even have a chance to get out of their sleeping bags; only Uncle Moshe was able to find shelter, and he was saved. When it was all over, he realized that his nightmare had turned into an even more horrific reality.

Uncle Moshe's life, and the lives of everyone in his family, would never be the same as they had been before the Yom Kippur War. Uncle Moshe couldn't hold down a job. Some nights he couldn't sleep at all, other nights he would scream and cry in his sleep. Aunt Farida, whose love for life and for her family was fierce, made sure the kids never sensed that anything was out of order. She cared for him selflessly, and made sure that his children respected him. Then, two years ago, Uncle Moshe's heart could no longer carry the weight of all those memories, and he died . Farida, who had looked after him for so many years, was left alone.

"*Ya'allah*, Noa, start eating," Farida urged. "The food is getting cold, and you haven't even touched it. *Ya'allah*, eat already, before it gets cold and becomes *jifa*- nobody wants to eat rotten food. Now, tell your Aunt Farida a little about Noa: how is she doing, and when will she get married already, with God's help?"

"Really, Aunt Farida," Noa said, her mouth full. "Get married?

Who exactly do you suggest I marry? I don't even have a serious boyfriend. You know that Barak and I broke up awhile ago."

"Do I know, of course I know. OK, I'll tell you the truth, you want the truth?" Farida hoped that Noa would be willing to listen to her. Farida had a definite opinion about this issue- she had definite opinions about every issue- and it was hard for her to keep her thoughts to herself.

"Sure, I want the truth, why not," Noa said, laying her fork down on the plate. She knew that nothing she could say would keep her aunt from telling her what she thought about Barak. She looked curiously at her aunt, and waited.

"He's all wrong for you," Farida said, dismissing him with a wave of her hands. "He loves himself too much, what can I tell you," she continued. "You need someone who will love you more than he loves himself. This young man is killing you."

"Right." Noa smiled. Aunt Farida's outlook on the world was unambiguous. Everything was either black or white; there was no such thing as grey. "In the meantime I am kissing lots of frogs," she said with a wink, "until I find a real prince."

"I pity those boys when you're around," Farida laughed. "Do they know that in your eyes, they're just frogs?" She let her plump arms fall to her sides. "So some day, one of these frogs will turn into a prince? I like that idea. Now that I think about it, most of the men that I've met in my life really were frogs. A couple of them were princes, including your father, God protect him. Do you know that I saw him yesterday at Uncle Anwar's house? He is a good man, your father. I hear he's taking a class in geography, and that sometimes the two of you meet between classes."

"Yes, that's true," Noa said. She went back to her food, surprised and relieved that the conversation about Barak was already over. "We do meet from time to time, and it's great that we have new topics to discuss. He's quite the student," she said proudly. "He never misses a lecture. You won't believe his latest kick: he wants to get a doctorate in geography- Ima's field- and complete her research."

"Are you serious? I had no idea. Good for him," Farida said

with admiration.

"You know, it's really nice to see him there," Noa said. "He looks much younger, all of a sudden. He's smiling again."

"Good," Farida said, "very good. I'm happy for him. It's time for him to start looking for a wife, don't you think?" She smiled mischievously at her niece.

"It is time, but you know how it is. At that age, it's not so simple."

"Tell me about it!" Farida said, and she looked at Noa. I understand, her eyes were saying. I'm in the same predicament.

All this talk of Noa's father, especially the part about his romantic life, made Noa uncomfortable. It wouldn't be easy seeing her father with a woman who wasn't her mother. She veered the conversation back to her aunt.

"So what's new with you, Aunt Farida?" Noa looked at her aunt's large hands. "Look how rude I'm being, I haven't even complimented you yet on your delicious okra. The crust is amazing. *Gute, gute,* like Grandmother used to say. It's just how I like it. We've been talking about me this whole time, and you haven't even told me what's going on in your life. What have you been up to lately? How are Sigali and the kids? I haven't seen them in ages."

"Bless God's name forever and ever, may his name be blessed, I can't complain," Farida said, staring at the kitchen ceiling and shaking her hands towards heaven. "Look, I'm keeping busy, as you can see. I couldn't even make it to the hairdresser, and tomorrow Sigali's taking half a day's vacation and bringing the kids for a visit. Can you believe that Ruthie's in second grade already? You should see this little slip of a girl reading and writing like the devil. And Shai is in his last year of pre-school, driving his teacher crazy. Did you know he has a male teacher this year?"

"What? A man teaching pre-school?"

"That's right. As you can see, you don't need boobs to go into this profession. He's a fantastic teacher," Farida said. "Yaron- that's his name- takes the kids out on nature walks and teaches them the names of plants. He knows all the songs, and on Pesach he taught the kids how to make wine by stomping on grapes."

"Nice," Noa agreed, impressed.

"But while we're on the subject of me," Farida said, eager to steer the conversation back to herself, "it's not easy living alone. The days are one thing, but the nights...." Farida eyes were full of anguish. "During the day I'm busy, but at night, if you want to know the truth, at night it's a whole other story." She tried to lean back in her chair, but her corpulent body kept sliding back and forth on the seat, and she couldn't get comfortable.

"I can't fall asleep at night." Farida wanted Noa to share the burden of her pain. "The nights go on forever- they have a beginning, but no end," she continued sadly. "I go to bed as late as I can"- she began counting on her fingers- "I watch all the late shows on all the channels, and still I can't fall asleep. Then I wander around the house all night, like a sleepwalker. I have no idea what's going on… maybe it's my age… maybe it's because summer's around the corner… or maybe it's the heat," she concluded. She looked at Noa's plate. "I see you ate it all, a blessing on your head, come, let's clean up and start baking," she said, trying to infuse the cramped kitchen with a more joyful spirit.

Aunt Farida stood up and walked over to the counter, which was covered with all kinds of delicious food. She picked up the huge platter that stood next to the neat rows of spices; then she leaned over heavily; a pair of thick legs peeked out from behind her house-dress. She began to rummage through one of the shelves. This was where she stored all her baking equipment, which she'd bought long ago. When they were done clearing the table, Farida put down the yeasty dough that had already risen. Taking pleasure in its appearance, in its very presence, she rolled it into a log and split it into two pieces, one of which she gave to Noa. The two women, one young, one old, sat by the table and rolled the dough into tiny balls. They were making s*ambusak bejiben*, a kind of cheese-filled pastry. Later on, part of the dough would be filled with dates and sprinkled with sesame seeds. These yeast cookies, or *baba*, would fill the room with their sweet smell. The women fell silent as they concentrated on their task. Each of them was focusing on her own work, engrossed in her own thoughts.

"From everything you're telling me," Noa said, returning to

their discussion of Aunt Farida's sleeplessness, "it sounds pretty serious. Maybe you should try warm milk, or taking deep breaths like they do in yoga."

"Nothing's going to help," Farida said, "it's awful. *Ya'allah*, forget it, there's no point in discussing it."

"Well, if we're pouring our hearts out," Noa began, "if we're talking about truth and feelings…." She spoke slowly, averting her eyes from her aunt's face, concentrating on her work, as if rolling out little balls of dough was the most important thing she'd ever done. "Lately I've been very distressed. I don't know what's going on."

"As soon as I saw your face in the doorway I knew that something was not right," Aunt Farida said, her genuine concern mingling with satisfaction. She raised her arms helplessly, then put her hands to her cheeks and shook her head from side to side, as if something catastrophic had occurred. "Why, my girl, a blessing on your head, why are you sad? What's missing in your life? Maybe you should go live with your father again? Maybe leaving home wasn't such a good idea? You had everything you could ask for when you were living there, plus now you've left your father all alone. I've been saying for a long time that living in an apartment by yourself was a mistake." She wagged her fingers. "If you lived at home, your father could take care of you. He could cook for you and do your laundry. What's so great about all this solitude, anyway?" She was speaking very quickly.

"Maybe, Aunt Farida. I've thought about it; we'll see." Noa was losing patience. She hadn't come here to hear lectures, and she certainly hadn't come here to upset her aunt. She drew in a deep breath, then continued more slowly. "It's not as simple as you think. I miss Ima so much, every day I long for her more," she said, lowering her eyes to the table. "I'm asking myself all these questions, and I'm not getting any answers. Do you understand?" Noa finally lifted her gaze, looking for the answer in her aunt's eyes. "I keep asking myself, where is she when I need her? I know it makes no sense."

"Not everything in life makes sense, Noa'le," Aunt Farida said kindly. "It is what it is, as the young people say," she added, half smiling.

"But do you understand? I feel like she disappeared too soon, like I don't know enough about her, her family, you, your childhood. Ima didn't talk much about her childhood. And I have my own feelings of guilt," Noa said, pointing to her heart. "I feel like maybe I wasn't there for her when she needed me," she muttered quickly, painfully, as if she were worried that if she slowed down and thought about what she wanted to say, she wouldn't be able to speak. Aunt Farida's love for Noa was absolute, and Noa knew that she could tell her anything. Aunt Farida would always understand, and would do whatever she could to ease Noa's pain.

"What? Why are you tormenting yourself?" This conversation was hard for her, and Aunt Farida was distracting herself by putting all her energy into rolling the dough into little balls. "You were in the army when your mother got sick. What could you have done?"

"It's true, I was in the army." Noa looked painfully into her aunt's face. She took a deep breath, and forced herself to examine the whole truth, all at once. Let it all out, she told herself. Don't keep anything inside your aching heart; tell Aunt Farida the whole thing before she has a chance to stop me. "I was in the army, but it was so selfish of me not to even try to be closer to Ima. I should have asked to serve closer to home, but instead I ran away from home, I ran away from the sickness, I couldn't stand looking at her deteriorating body. Her beautiful face that looked more and more sunken every time I saw her, like her eyes were about to meet, like her cheeks were stuck together. I couldn't stand the way she tried to convince me that everything was fine, that she was strong. I knew there was no chance she'd get out of this, that it was just a matter of time. I can't live with these thoughts all the time, do you understand?" Tears streamed down her cheeks.

"Do you understand?" Noa caught her breath, then continued. "I wanted to get used to her absence before she was even gone. I tried to see what it was like to live without her, and the whole time I knew that when it got to be too much, I'd have a place to go, and she'd always welcome me with a smile. I didn't think about *her*," she said wretchedly. "I didn't think about how hard it was for her, don't you see?" She repeated herself, hoping that her aunt would understand everything she was saying. "I only thought about myself," she said again, pointing her index finger at herself, jabbing it into her ribs. "I never thought about Ima's separation from me. I never thought about how I wasn't there on a daily basis. I separated from her while she was still with us, and I didn't take advantage of the time we had left. And for that," she concluded in anguish, "I can never forgive myself."

"Oh, my child," Aunt Farida said, taking Noa's two hands in her own warm hands. "Now listen to me, listen very closely. Your mother was glad that you were busy, that you had a full and busy life, and that you were a successful officer. At first she was sad when you went into the army, but when she saw how good it was for you, she was happy for you. And when you became the first officer in our family, your mother was so proud, she talked about it all the time. The truth is, she was relieved that you didn't see her suffer. She wanted to shield you from her pain; she knew how hard her illness was on you. Your mother talked about you all the time, she told me everything you told her, every detail. And to every detail, she added on her own blessings. Your mother didn't expect you, a girl of nineteen, to sit with her all day and watch her suffer. You're a kind and sensitive soul, Noa'le, your mother would have been just as proud of you today. It's good that you think about her, that you miss her. It's good, my girl. But sadness?" She stroked Noa's face. "What a waste," she said, "really, that's no good. Oh, the *sambusk* is burning, I'd better take it out of the oven." She shuffled over to the oven to take out the dessert, which was truly on the verge of ruin.

Noa looked at her aunt and tried to digest all that she had just heard. There were so many things that she hadn't known. Noa hadn't known that her mother had understood her, or that she hadn't been angry with her. She was struck by how much she didn't know about her mother.

After she took the pastries out of the oven, Aunt Farida stood behind Noa and stroked her long hair. "Shhh… shhh… it's alright," she whispered softly into Noa's ear. "Everything's alright, my child, my dear one. It's good that you told me all these things," she continued, trying to revive Noa's spirits. "It's good to cry, to let it all out. You know that I'm always here for you, my darling, no matter what... How did we get to the point of tears? You must have been thinking about these things for a long time."

Aunt Farida walked over to the other side of Noa, so she could see her niece's face. She leaned forward, and took her niece's hands into her own. Her voice was gentle. "Now listen very carefully to what I'm about to tell you. You're a big girl now, you're independent. You're everything your mother wanted you to be, ever since you were in the womb. She wanted a girl exactly like you: sensitive, smart, thoughtful, loving. Even when you were a little girl, you made your mother so proud. And I know that your mother, of blessed memory, is looking down at you now and thinking about what a good job she did raising you. You're an adult now, you're strong." She started speaking more slowly. "And for that reason, for that very reason...." She was repeating herself, considering her words carefully before she spoke them out loud. "It's for that reason that I can now give you something that I couldn't give you before."

"What is it, Aunt Farida? What do you want to give me?" Noa's eyes were wide.

"Your mother's diary," Farida said quietly.

A heavy silence fell upon the room. Noa shook off her aunt's hands, and wiped her eyes. When she spoke, her voice was a combination of surprise and fury. "A diary... what kind of diary? What are you talking about, since when was there a diary? Why didn't you tell me about this sooner? How dare you hide this from me?" Noa couldn't believe her ears, and, even worse, she felt cheated by the person who had been her protector all her life. She stormed out of the kitchen, shocked and angry.

Farida rose, too, as though someone had stuck a pin in her behind. She stood up so quickly she even surprised herself, and stumbled after Noa into the small living room. "Noa, Noa, my girl, don't be angry at me. You have to understand. Just wait a minute," she pleaded. She reached out to take her niece's hand, but Noa refused to touch her, and Farida stepped back.

"You tell me, Noa'le," Farida said. "How could I have given a twenty-year old girl, a girl who didn't know anything about life, the diary of her mother who had just died? You weren't mature enough; you weren't ready. Even without the diary, it wasn't easy for you." She was pleading with her niece. "To read things about one's mother, that's not easy for a daughter, especially one whose mother had just died. So we waited, your father and I, we waited for you to grow up, we waited until you were ready to read the diary, and to understand it. I wanted to give you the diary when *you* came to *me,* just like you did today, when you started looking for answers about who your mother really was, when you started looking for your roots. I wanted it to come from you, not from me or your father or anyone else. Do you understand what I'm saying?" Her voice was full of pain.

"So you and Aba, the two of you were in this together?" Noa shot back. She felt like everyone in the entire world knew about this, everyone except her.

"A blessing on your head." Farida tried to diffuse the situation. "Your father and I were the only ones who knew about your mother's diary, and we decided not to tell anyone else about it because we didn't want you and Guy to feel like the whole world was hiding something from you. Listen," Farida said, once again trying to put her hand on Noa's shoulder, and once again being rebuffed. "When your mother started writing, she had no idea what would happen to her. Listen to me very carefully: in the beginning your mother wrote only for herself, that's what she told me. It's not easy being sick, and writing in her diary was a way for her to express her feelings. Later on, though, she wrote for you."

Farida gazed deeply into Noa's eyes, and raised her hands to the heavens. "Do you understand? Your mother, God have mercy on her soul, kept this diary for you and for Guy. She made your father and me swear that we wouldn't give it to you until you were a little older. Those were her exact words. She said to me, 'Farida, I'm counting on you and Dan to give this diary to Noa only when you're sure that she can appreciate what's inside.'"

Noa's expression softened a bit, and Farida continued.

"This diary, it has everything she ever wanted to tell you. She wanted you to know, that's what she told me, may I fall down dead if I'm not telling the truth. Some of the stories you've already heard, from me or from her, but your mother wanted you to learn about her whole life. She wanted you to know the story of our family. She thought that when you had families of your own, you'd want to know, but that until then you were too young to care. Someday, she thought, you might want to know more, and who knew if she'd be around to tell you yourself. Those were her exact words. So please understand"- she reached out for Noa's hand, and this time Noa didn't flinch- "it was for your own good. It was never my intention to take this diary to the grave. Basically, I was just waiting for the right moment, and now that moment has come. Do you see now?" She was practically shouting. It hadn't been easy for Farida to keep the diary a secret. From the time she and Dan were entrusted with the diary, she had often been tempted to give it to Noa, and there were times when she and Dan almost did, but neither of them thought that the time was right. Now, Farida felt, the time had come.

"I don't believe this," Noa cried out. Again, tears flooded her eyes, choked her throat. "I want to see this diary! Where is it? Where did you put it? And anyway," she added, "why do you have it in the first place?"

Chapter Five: Farida

After Noa left, Farida stood at the kitchen window for a long time, looking out into the black, moonless night. Hoping it would relieve her anxiety, she lit a cigarette, one of the cheap Silons that were so hard to find, and she leaned heavily against the window, as if she could no longer carry her own weight. She drew the smoke into her lungs and tried to calm her mind. Uncharacteristically, she let the dirty dishes sit, even though she had finished her cooking and baking. The table was full of silverware, the floor was covered with a thin film of flour, and the sink was overflowing with the dishes she and Noa had just used.

She considered how Noa would be affected by the diary. Doubts began to creep into her mind. Dan had entrusted her with the diary years ago; she had asked for it. They passed it back and forth, depending on who needed it more. Each time the precious notebook was passed from one person to the other, they reaffirmed their commitment: when the time was right, they would give the diary to Noa. Although Farida's intuition never betrayed her, this time she was seized by doubt. She wasn't convinced that Noa would be able to read the diary and to truly understand its meaning. She wanted Noa to learn about her mother's life, about her roots, but she wasn't sure her niece was mature enough to appreciate the beauty of her mother's culture. Her hope was that the diary would make Noa feel closer to her mother, and in the process ease some of Noa's pain. Nonetheless, Farida worried that perhaps she shouldn't have given Noa the diary when she was so tormented, so caught up in her own thoughts. Perhaps she should have waited. On the other hand, maybe the diary was exactly what Noa needed in order to find some peace. Maybe now was when she most needed to know more about her mother, maybe the diary would answer some of Noa's questions.... The thoughts raced wildly through Farida's head, and she was unable to reach any conclusion.

From this jumble of thoughts, her sister's image arose before her eyes. Farida Sasson thought about Violet. It had been six years without her, and her absence was still so acute. She and Violet, the youngest daughters of the family... Violet was only slightly older, but in her relationship with Farida, she played the role of a much older sister. And they were always together: wherever Farida was, Violet was sure to be, and vice versa. Violet was the family rebel, and Farida always tagged along. As children, they had shared a room; they were together in the kibbutz, first in a tent and later on in a small apartment. As young girls in Baghdad, when Farida would lie awake through the long, cold, dusty winter nights, Violet would tell her sad stories about lovers who couldn't be together, or about a lame and lonely dog searching for affection, or about the desert bandits who roamed by night and attacked by day.

In the desert, the winter mornings were bitterly cold, inside the house as well as outside. Violet, an early riser, would climb out of bed, get dressed, brush her teeth, and go downstairs to make sandwiches for her and Farida to take to school. Then she would pick out clothes for her younger sister, bring them to their room, climb into Farida's bed, and keep her warm until she was completely dressed. Then she would comb her sister's hair, and the two of them would go off to school. Whenever they were late- which was often, since Farida always wanted to stay in her warm bed for just one more minute- Violet would beg the guard to let her little sister go into school, and she would remain outside, bearing the punishment by herself.

When Farida thought about her sister, she could feel her standing right there. She could feel the touch of her sister's soft, kind hands. She closed her eyes and succumbed to the feeling of her sister's lips kissing her head, protecting her even now. Violet shouldn't have left this world the way she did, Farida thought bitterly. Violet was the symbol of a joyful family life, with a smile forever dancing playfully on her lips.

What a miserable, heartbreaking end her beloved sister Violet had met, thought Farida. And now, what was left in this world? Violet was gone, Eddie was gone, and her own Moshe had passed on two years ago. How much pain could one person endure in life and still get out of bed every morning? Farida was overcome by a searing loneliness; her own generation was dying out, the younger generation was growing increasingly distant, everyone was busy with their own problems, and what would become of her? Slowly, she made her way over to the armchair on the front porch and parachuted herself into it. With a deep sigh, she lit another cigarette and leaned back. Tomorrow was a new day. Tomorrow the grandchildren would come. A tiny smile crossed her lips when she thought about the two noisy children whose laughter would fill the emptiness in her apartment, and the emptiness in her heart.

Chapter Six: Violet

Wednesday October 17, 1986

"The Waiting Period"

The ten days that followed my father's decree- my "Ten Days of Repentance"- were not all that bad. I spent my time daydreaming, and getting excited.: my nephew Eddie's Bar Mitzvah was fast approaching. I counted off the days with tremendous excitement. Eddie was thirteen… hard to believe. He was growing up. I wondered whether he would still play with me and Farida. For both of us, Eddie was the object of our adoration. His kindness, his intelligence, his wildness, and all his other magnificent characteristics, swept us off our feet. I was one year younger than him and one and a half years older that Farida, and the two of them were my whole world.

Eddie, Eddie, Eddie. Whenever I think of him, my heart aches with the same intensity as when we found out that we had lost him.

Eddie always knew exactly what to say. He was the only one of the kids who was allowed to go to the movies by himself (we were girls, and the other boys in the family were too young), and when he returned from a film, he would describe every scene, every detail. Eddie created his own movies, too, just for us. He'd cut out images from the newspaper and project them onto a screen that he had built himself; the images flowed so smoothly that we felt like we were watching a real movie. He even sewed a cloth curtain to cover the screen, which he removed only after we were all sitting down, breathlessly waiting for the movie to begin. He even prepared a snack for intermission: something sweet that his mother, or our mother, had made for him.

Eddie had a marvelous sense of humor, an uncanny memory for jokes, and a gift for impersonation. He would imitate the teachers at school, he would even imitate Ima's friends… nobody could resist his magic. Whenever I cried, Eddie made me laugh, and when I was bored, he riled me up. He was my best friend, and he, Farida and I made a joyful trio.

When the evening before the big event finally arrived, we stood on the roof and kept a vigilant watch for my father's sister, Aunt Madeline, and for my grandmother, may she rest in peace.

Grandmother- I must write about her- was unique. When she was young, and her kids were still small, my grandfather was sent to fight against the Turks in World War One, and although he came back alive, he wasn't the same man. He had contracted tuberculosis, and he could no longer take care of his family. He died at a young age, when my father was just a boy. My grandmother, a young woman raising three small children, did her best to support her little family.

During the war, Grandmother raised chickens in her backyard. She used some of their eggs to feed her children, and the rest she sold. On rare occasions, they would eat the bird itself. When she realized that she couldn't support the family with chickens alone, Grandmother went out and bought inexpensive jewelry, material, and lacework. At night she sewed garments, and during the day she would go from house to house peddling her wares.

Grandmother traveled through the villages on foot, her merchandise packed on the back of a donkey; she frequently encountered vicious highway robbers. Whenever she heard about a celebration in one family or another, she would find out what the mother wished for, and she would make that wish come true. For one woman, she sewed a dreamlike wedding gown based on a drawing in a British magazine, and for someone else, she made a ballgown out of lace and muslin. She made clothes for men and children as well. I must point out that in those days, women like my grandmother were considered peculiar; wandering through the villages and selling one's wares was not thought of as suitable work for women. Those women who did make a living this way were looked upon as social outcasts, but my grandmother wasn't thinking about honor and status; she was thinking about how to feed her children. She didn't want to be a burden on her family, which was poor to start with.

During my grandmother's era, most widows ended up penniless. Even those who were left with a little bit of property were soon destitute, since they had no income aside from what their husband had left them. But Grandmother wasn't like other women. Circumstances, you could say, made her into a feminist. In addition to the financial hardships, tragedy seemed to pursue her. Grandmother lost her oldest son when an oil lamp set his robe on fire. My father, her second son, started accompanying my grandmother at a young age, traveling with her, helping her carry her goods. When he grew up, he opened a small store and sold their wares.

My mother, a strong, proud woman, never forgave my father's mother for her low social status. She herself came from a rabbinic family on one side, and a wealthy family on the other. Although my father was learned, he was not worthy of my mother, and as for this old and simple woman who would be her mother-in-law… well, that was too much to bear. My mother didn't see any good in her. She tended to look more at the envelope than at the letter inside…. For my part, I loved my kind grandmother, and now, with the wisdom of years, I can say that she was in fact worthy of admiration.

My father spoke seven languages *al burian,* fluently. While he was working with my grandmother, he decided to study business administration. He was quite talented, and was hired by the government for a high-ranking position. In Iraq of the 1930's and 40's, being a civil servant was honorable work, second only to doctors and bank officers. My father, who was a very quick thinker, was granted the coveted position, and he stayed there for many years, until the birth of the State of Israel. Many Jews lost their jobs with the establishment of the Jewish state, not just him. In any case, my father won my mother's heart, partly because of his intelligence, and partly because he knew how to play the *ud-* the fat-bellied guitar that was so popular in those days.

My mother selected her own husband, which was not the custom back then. Traditionally, the girl's parents would choose a groom for their daughter. My mother, the eldest daughter of the most learned and revered man in the village, liked to say that she had grown up "on a silver platter." Her father- my grandfather- admired his daughter's cleverness, and worshiped the ground on which she walked. He would ask her for advice, and take her opinion into consideration. In the end, my mother never forgave herself for marrying someone from such a lowly family. When they were living in Baghdad, she still showed him some respect, but all that changed when they moved to Israel, and she- who was used to a life of luxury- was forced to live in a tent, and later in a crowded apartment.

Back to that long-ago night: from everything you've just read, you can probably understand why I saw Grandmother so infrequently. I admired Grandmother, and I loved her. She had life experience. She would tell spellbinding stories about her travels in the villages, and amusing stories about all the different women she met and all the thieves she eluded. She was warm and open-hearted, and best of all, she would sew me the most magnificent dresses, with muslin trim, all in the latest London fashion. Because of this, I always longed for her visits. My father's sister Madeline, on the other hand, I didn't like at all. Aunt Madeline was conceited, and she considered children bothersome. I think I disliked her primarily because of the infamous story, the stain on our family's name: she insulted my mother by rejecting her dowry.

Young people today, at the end of the second millennium, have a hard time grasping the magnitude of the insult, but in Iraqi families, the custom was for the bride to give her in-laws a dowry that her parents had been saving for from the day she was born. My mother's parents worked especially hard, since she was their first daughter after they had lost the baby. Iraq in the early 1900's didn't have the same health standards we have today, and a lot of babies died either at birth or soon after. As the oldest daughter, my mother was the apple of her father's eye; in fact, the entire family doted upon her. My grandfather invested a great deal in her dowry. He made sure it was a lavish one, with elegant furniture, napkins woven with lace and gold, summer and winter curtains, anything a young couple might dream of for their new home. After being loaded on a large wagon, the dowry made its way to the groom's home for approval.

The glorious dowry of *Bint Ruven-* the daughter of Reuven- was sent off with a flurry of trills from all the neighbors, Arab and Jewish alike. It traveled from the poor side of the Jewish neighborhood to the rich side. Aunt Madeline, who was jealous and bitter and had never made a life for herself, who never had a family of her own, who always tagged along with my father, decided that the dowry was insufficient. Without telling my grandfather, she sent it back to my grandparents' house. The whole way back, the neighbors looked on and figured out what had happened. They beat their chests and shrieked, "*Ya buya, Ya buya,* something terrible has happened, they've broken up!" The rejection of a dowry was considered a grave insult, and my mother never forgave my aunt for this abasement. After an abject apology from my father's parents, after they had ironed out all the misunderstandings, after they had utterly ingratiated themselves… only then did the wedding preparation resume. Right before the wedding, my father got a job in Baghdad- the big city. My mother was relieved; she wouldn't have to see the face of her evil sister-in-law on a daily basis, or those of her brazen parents-in-law.

I'm glad I got all this down on paper. One day, this will take on a different meaning to the young generation that knew nothing about life in Iraq. I feel compelled to write all this for the sake of future generations. If my generation doesn't tell the story of "The Exodus out of Iraq," nothing will be known about our culture, nothing will remain. But now I'm tired. I'll write more another time.

Daughters of Iraq is available in paperback and in eBook formats online.

ABOUT THE AUTHOR

Revital Shiri-Horowitz was born and raised in Israel. She immigrated to the United States after her first son was born. Shiri-Horowitz has written two novels. **Daughters of Iraq**, a historical fiction based on her family. It won an award from The Jewish Iraqi Heritage Center, (2011). Her second book **Hope to See You Soon** (2014) speaks about immigrants, always divided between two homelands. **It's Just Your Imagination** is her third book.

www.ingramcontent.com/pod-product-compliance
Lightning Source LLC
LaVergne TN
LVHW011839060526
838200LV00054B/4098